# PUPPY
# Start Right

## FOUNDATION TRAINING FOR THE COMPANION DOG

Kenneth M. Martin, DVM
Debbie Martin, RVT, VTS (Behavior), CPDT-KA, KPA CTP

karen
pryor
CLICKER TRAINING

Puppy Start Right
Foundation Training for the Companion Dog

Karen Pryor Clicker Training
49 River Street, Suite 3
Waltham, MA 02453 USA

www.clickertraining.com


For information about special discounts for multiple-copy
purchases please contact Karen Pryor Clickertraining sales
at +1 781-398-0754 or wholesale@clickertraining.com.

First edition published 2009
Second edition 2011

Printed in the United States of America

20 19 18 17 16


ISBN-10: 1-890948-44-6

ISBN-13: 978-1-890948-44-3


Library of Congress Control Number: 2011944959

# Table of Contents

# PREFACE

This book was designed as a scientifically based and dog-friendly resource regarding behavior and training. **Puppy Start Right** provides the foundation for a lifelong partnership with your dog based on mutual trust and understanding.

Unfortunately, many currently available resources provide misinformation regarding dog training and behavior. Much of the information refers to leadership and dominance for structuring our relationship with dogs. This information is not scientifically based and ultimately can be damaging to the human-animal bond.

Our goal is to provide a compact, yet comprehensive, user-friendly resource for the new puppy owner, as well as, the adult dog owner. For simplicity, in the text, dogs are referred to in the male gender. You may read the book in the order the chapters are presented or skip ahead and jump right into training. The book is not intended to be all encompassing and does not address the treatment of behavior disorders.

Behavioral disorders differ from training problems. A behavioral disorder is an emotional disorder relating to aggression, fear, or anxiety. Training alone does not improve behavioral disorders. Training problems relate to a lack of response to "human taught" cues or commands. Dogs that are behaviorally normal and emotionally stable yet lack basic manners related to walking on leash, coming when called, sitting, lying down, and staying, fit into the category of a training problem. Training problems are common in young and adolescent dogs. This book addresses behavior disorder prevention and foundation training.

If you are concerned your dog has a behavioral disorder, you should contact your veterinarian. Information on how to contact qualified animal behavior professionals is located in the appendix.

Prevention of behavior problems through appropriate early training and management helps to keep pets in their home. One study reports that 4 million dogs are relinquished to animal shelters, 2 million are euthanized, and 7.7 million (15%) of owned dogs change their homes annually.[1] Other studies report relinquishment numbers as high as 20 million. Pet overpopulation is largely due to a high demand for puppies and relinquishment of adolescent dogs. The number one reason for relinquishment is behavior or training problems. Many of these problem behaviors can be prevented with early socialization and foundation training.

The purpose of this book is to foster the human-animal bond and decrease pet relinquishment through education about normal behavior, prevention, problem solving, and humane training. We dedicate this book not only to improving the welfare of dogs, but the families who love them.

*Kenneth and Debbie Martin*

## Reference

1.   Patronek, G., Glickman, L. et al. Risk factors for relinquishment of dogs to an animal shelter, *J. Amer. Vet. Med. Assoc.*, 209:572–581, 1996.

# ACKNOWLEDGMENTS

We would like to thank Andrew Luescher, DVM, PhD, DACVB, DECVBM and Julie Shaw, RVT. Their mentorship, knowledge, and guidance have been instrumental in the writing of this book.

We would like to acknowledge friends and family members who have been supportive in reviewing and commenting on drafts of this book.

Thank you to all the dogs with whom we have shared our homes and lives, as well as clients and clients' dogs we have had the pleasure of meeting. Learning is a continuous process, and we strive to learn something new with each dog and person we encounter.

Veterinary Behavior Consultations, LLC
2330 Somerset Drive
New Orleans, LA 70131

# GROWING UP

## Developmental Periods

Developmental periods are critical or sensitive stages for behavioral development and learning. Within these early finite stages of development are optimal periods for stimulus contact, environmental exposure, and social experience. Stages of development are guidelines. Different breeds will transition from developmental stages at slightly different rates. From 3 to 16 weeks of age, puppies probably learn more than they do during the remaining course of their lifetime, forming lasting lifelong cognitive and emotional impressions. [1]

**Key points:**

- There are 8 developmental periods: prenatal, neonatal, transitional, socialization, juvenile, adolescent, adult, and senior.
- Dogs will transition through the developmental periods at slightly different rates.
- The mother's nutritional and emotional state has an impact on fetal development.

| TABLE 1.1 CANINE DEVELOPMENTAL PERIODS | |
|---|---|
| Prenatal | In utero |
| Neonatal | Birth to 12 days |
| Transitional | 12 days to 3 weeks |
| Socialization | 3 weeks to 12 weeks (< 16 weeks) |
| Juvenile | 12 weeks to sexual maturity |
| Adolescent | Sexual to social maturity |
| Adult | Social maturity to 7 + years |
| Senior | 7 + years |

### Prenatal

The mother's nutritional and emotional state has an impact on fetal development. Proper maternal nutrition is necessary for the developing fetus. If the mother is repeatedly exposed to fear-inducing stimuli while pregnant, the puppies are more likely to be emotionally unstable and reactive.

Testosterone masculinizes the male brain and pending uterine position may masculinize the female brain.[2] In utero exposure to testosterone may produce male like tendencies such as leg lifting and male-directed aggression in adult female dogs.

### Neonatal (Infant)

Puppies are blind and deaf during the neonatal period. Sensory perception is limited to temperature, pressure, movement, taste, and smell. Similar to human infants, puppies are dependent on their mother for survival. Urination and defecation must be elicited by the mother licking the anogenital region. Most of a puppy's time is spent sleeping with the remainder of the time nursing. Rudimentary learning of an approach-withdrawal response is present at birth. Neonates show an avoidance response to painful stimuli and noxious odors. External influences have a long-term effect on behavior and development. Neonatal puppies should be handled and exposed to mild environmental stressors, such as changes in surface texture and temperature. Stimulation for as little as 3 minutes a day has a positive impact on a puppy's resistance to disease, emotional reactivity, and adult learning and problem solving ability.[3, 4]

### Transitional (Toddler)

Puppies become more active and independent with progressive sensory and neurological development. Puppies may begin to walk unsteadily as early as day 12. Their eyes open early (12 to 14 days) within this stage, but their vision is poor. Later during this period, their ears open (20 to 21 days) and teeth emerge (19 to 20 days). Elimination behavior occurs independently of maternal stimulation. The desire for social contact is greater than nursing. Puppies weaned prior to day 15 are predisposed to developing adult compulsive behaviors involving the sucking and kneading of objects.[5] Developing neurologic and sensory abilities dramatically influence the puppy's ability to learn. **Novel stimuli should be introduced to the whelping box during this time.**

**Key points:**

- Early neonatal handling (as little as 3 minutes a day) and exposure to various mild environmental stressors is beneficial.

- During the transition period, puppies become more active and independent with progressive sensory and neurological development..

Transitional stage Shetland sheepdog (14 days old). The eyes have opened, but vision is not completely developed.

## Socialization (Preschooler)

The socialization period is a critical period of development whereby a dog learns to communicate and relate to other dogs, humans, and the environment. It is the most influential learning period of a dog's life, forming the foundation for all future learning. Socialization can be divided into primary socialization (3 to 5 weeks of age) and secondary socialization (6 to 12 weeks of age). Lack of exposure and positive experiences during this time will prevent the puppy from reaching its full potential. Foundation training should begin during the socialization period at 8 weeks of age. Based on EEG (electroencephalogram) and multiple behavioral studies, the brain is adult-like at 8 weeks of age, and puppies function at an adult level in terms of learning ability.[6]

> A **Fear Period** has been documented to occur between 8 to 10 weeks of age.[7] Traumatic experiences to stimuli that induce fear during this sensitive period may be generalized and produce lifelong aversion responses. **Puppies should not be shipped during this period, elective surgery should be put off until after the 12th week, and veterinary visits should be made positive with treats.**

Socialization vaccinates your puppy against behavior problems. Similarly, expect to take your puppy to your veterinarian every 3 to 4 weeks during this period for vaccinations against infectious disease. Many adult behavior problems can be prevented or reduced through appropriate and thorough socialization. This is such an important stage of development that an entire chapter has been dedicated to this topic (Chapter 4: Socialization).

## Juvenile (Elementary Age)

This period begins with the end of the socialization period and ends at sexually maturity (approximately 6 to 9 months of age). The end of the juvenile period is a common time when dogs are spayed or neutered. Puppies become progressively more independent as juveniles. Stabilization of social dominance amongst littermates that remain together occurs between 10 to 16 weeks of age. As puppies mature, the ease of learning begins to decline by about 16 weeks of age.[8] Permanent teeth begin to emerge by 4 months of age. The optimal time for social and environmental exposure is prior to 16 weeks of age, yet socialization during the juvenile period and beyond is still beneficial and necessary. Discontinuance of socialization beyond the socialization period will cause dogs to regress and become fearful. Between 12 weeks of age and 16 weeks of age, puppies become progressively more reluctant to approach novelty and unfamiliar people without apprehension and fear responses.

**Key points:**

- The socialization period is the most important period of development pertaining to the prevention of future behavior disorders.

- A fear period occurs between 8 and 10 weeks of age.

- Traumatic events during fear periods can have a profound impact on future behavior.

- Socialization vaccinates your puppy against behavior problems.

- Puppies in the juvenile period become progressively more fearful and reluctant to approach novelty and unfamiliar people.

Adolescent dogs (like teenagers) left unsupervised are likely to get into trouble. What happens when two adolescent Belgian Malinois are not closely supervised? Goodbye therapeutic pillow!

**Key points:**

- Training and behavior problems are likely to become more pronounced in the adolescent period.

- During adolescence, puppies become skeletally mature, but they are not yet socially mature.

- Dogs experience a second fear period during adolescence.

## Adolescent (Teenager)

This developmental period ranges from sexual maturity to social maturity (2 to 3 years of age). Sexual maturing coincides with puberty (the first female heat cycle, or increase in male testosterone). Males may start lifting their legs to urine mark at sexual maturity. Skeletal maturity coincides with closure of the growth plates. This typically occurs at about 8 to 10 months of age in medium-size dogs (adult weight of approximately 50 pounds). Your dog will acquire all of his permanent adult teeth during this stage. Think of your dog as a teenager. He may be skeletally and sexually mature, but he is not yet socially mature. Ideally, foundation training has already commenced because your dog is becoming bigger and more independent everyday. Consistency and predictability in your behavior is important during this phase. It is important to keep training sessions short and fun. Prevention and management of behaviors that are not under your control will keep your dog from learning unwanted behaviors. Physical and mental exercise for your dog will be essential to making this stage more enjoyable. Training problems and behavior disorders are likely to become more pronounced during this stage of development. For example, dogs may start barking at strangers entering the home or become territorial during adolescence.

A **Second Fear Period** between 6 and 14 months of age and lasting for 1 to 3 weeks has been suggested by Michael Fox.[9] Adolescent dogs may be apprehensive or fearful of familiar and unfamiliar stimuli. Although not as critical as the first fear period, traumatic events should be avoided during this time.

## Adult

Dogs become socially mature at 2 to 3 years of age. Small-breed dogs will mature faster than large-breed dogs. Play behavior may decrease as dogs reach social maturity. As dogs become socially mature, they are more confident because they are in their physical and mental prime. Dominance and subordinate relationships amongst dogs living in the same household may change when dogs reach social maturity.

Adult dogs should receive veterinary wellness exams at least annually. Your veterinarian is a valuable resource for preventative care and the optimal maintenance of your dog's health. Vaccination protocols are based on state and local ordinances, your dog's exposure risk, and your veterinarian's recommendations. Generally, your dog will be vaccinated every 1 to 3 years against infectious diseases.

## Senior

Dogs become senior at 7+ years of age. Small-breed dogs, with an increased longevity, become senior at a greater age (10 to 12 years of age), when compared to large-breed dogs. As dogs age, their activity level may decrease. This may be associated with degenerative processes such as arthritis, reduced hearing, normal clouding of the cornea and/or reduced visual acuity, and muscle atrophy. Senior dogs should be screened at least annually by a veterinarian for medical disorders, as well as behavioral changes associated with aging. Some senior dogs will develop cognitive dysfunction syndrome, similar to human Alzheimer's disease or dementia. Early medical and behavioral treatment can greatly benefit the welfare of these dogs. Mental stimulation in the form of play and training is important for physical and behavioral wellness of all senior dogs.

**Key points:**

- Your puppy's true personality may not be known until he is socially mature or adult-like at 2 to 3 years of age.

- Senior dogs may develop health and behavior problems associated with normal and abnormal age-related changes.

# References

1.  Scott JP. 1958. Critical periods in the development of social behavior in puppies. *Psychosom Med,* 20:42–54.

2.  Knol BW and Egberink-Alink ST. 1989. Treatment of problem behavior in dogs and cats by castration and progestagen administration: A review. *Vet Q*, 11:102–107.

3.  Morton JRC. 1968. Effects of early experience "handling and gentling" in laboratory animals. In: MW Fox (Ed), Abnormal Behavior in Animals. Philadelphia: WB Saunders.

4.  Lindsay SR. 2000. Handbook of applied dog behavior and training. Volume 1, First edition. Iowa State University Press. pp 36–37.

5.  Knol BW and Egberink-Alink ST. 1989. Treatment of problem behavior in dogs and cats by castration and progestagen administration: A review. *Vet Q*, 11:102–107.

6.  Lindsay SR. 2000. Handbook of applied dog behavior and training. Volume 1, First edition. Iowa State University Press. p 63.

7.  Fox MW. 1966. Neuro-behavioral ontogeny: A synthesis of ethological and neurophysiological concepts. *Brain Res*, 2:3–20.

8.  Scott JP and Fuller JL, 1965. Genetics and the social behavior of the dog. Chicago: University of Chicago Press.

9.  Fox MW. 1978. Socialization patterns in wild and domesticated canids (ch.8), Stages and periods in development: environmental influences and domestication (ch.9), in *The Dog; Its Domestication and Behavior*, New York & London: Garland STPM Press, pp 141–152, 153–176.

# CHAPTER 2

# FROM WOLVES TO DOGS

## Domestication

Domestication of the gray wolf (Canis lupus) took place approximately 15,000 years ago in central Asia.[1] Although it is possible that dogs were domesticated earlier, there is little evidence of morphological (form and structural) differences from wolves.[2] The domestic dog (Canis lupus familiaris) is the product of co-evolution and co-domestication. Voluntary association between wolves and human settlements benefitted both parties. At times, each was dependant on the other for survival. Initially, environmental factors and functional roles shaped their morphology and behavior. In the last few hundred years, through selective breeding, humans have developed the varied breeds of dog that are known today.

Dogs were selectively bred for neoteny; they maintain juvenile characteristics into adulthood. Morphologically, these characteristics include a soft coat, curled tail, skin folds, floppy ears, and short legs. Behaviorally, dogs remain puppy-like, engaging in social play and barking, throughout their lifetimes. These puppy-like characteristics only occur in juvenile wolves; they do not occur in adult wolves. These juvenile characteristics make it possible for us to share our homes with domestic dogs. Through progressive selection for tameness, and against predatory behavior and aggression, the domestic dog is what it is today.

## Social Behavior

Invariably, morphologically and behaviorally, the domestic dog is far removed from its predecessor, the gray wolf. The social system of wolves is based on highly ritualized conflict and a proposed linear "social dominance" hierarchy, although recent research describes wolves as role oriented rather than dominance or status oriented.[3] Members of the pack are interrelated; they grew up together, hunt cooperatively together, and share a common phenotype (they look and act alike). Intra-species aggression that results in injury is rare, as it decreases a pack's chances of survival. Wolves spend most of their lives in stable family groups which normally do not incorporate outsiders.[4, 5]

Domestic dogs form loose, temporary groups and/or interact fleetingly with other dogs during outings with humans.[6, 7] The social system of the domestic dog is much more fluid than that of wolves. Feral dogs show little of the complex social structure or dominance hierarchy proposed in wolf packs. For dogs, other members of their kind are of no help in locating food items, and are likely viewed as competitors.[8]

**Key points:**

- The domestic dog is the product of co-evolution and co-domestication of the gray wolf.

- Dogs display neoteny; they maintain juvenile characteristics into adulthood.

- Social behavior of domestic dogs is fluid and very different from wolves.

Resources for the domestic dog in the human domestic environment are constantly changing compared to resources present in the social system of wolves. Resources for wolves include food, sleeping areas, possessions, and breeding privileges. These resources are sources of social competition and when stable, provide the construct for a linear social hierarchy. Linear dominance hierarchies are difficult to construct in domestic dogs because of variation within a group of dogs and affiliations with dogs outside of the group. A group of dogs must stay together long enough for a statistical pattern to emerge. More than likely, domestic dogs do not form social hierarchies in the same way as wolves, and those hierarchies do not transcend species or include humans.

Variable resources in the human domestic environment include people, other pets, resting locations, feeding locations, toys, and food-based items. Social affiliations with people, dogs, and other pets may fluctuate daily, or at different developmental life stages in the typical human household as resources come and go in the environment. Fluidity of resources produces instability of inter-dog social relationships. The domestic dog faces more social challenges and must adapt to the fluidity of the ever-changing human world.

The social construct of the wolf pack is invariably different from that of the domestic dog. Phenotypic variation of domestic dog breeds affects body structures used for signaling and communicating between dogs. Puppies of domestic dogs who are removed from the litter at an early age (prior to 6 weeks of age) or who are not socialized with various different breeds at an early age often lack proper social communication skills. Lack of social skills contributes to miscommunication and may result in inter-dog aggression. Lack of learned bite inhibition during primary socialization often leads to bites that produce physical injury.

The relationship between dog and human is an affectionate relationship. Dogs often prefer human contact over contact with con-specifics (other dogs) when given the choice.[9, 10] Domestic dogs exhibit different play behavior when interacting with humans as opposed to con-specifics.[11] Humans and dogs share similar social needs; we live in groups, and enjoy social interaction. Dogs and humans each have their own unique and complex communication systems. Problems can arise in our relationships with our dogs due to miscommunication or in the viewing of our relationship in terms of dominance and submission. Fortunately, domestic dogs do not view humans as con-specifics in which to dominate. We often draw conclusions, wrongfully, about our dog's behavior based on human communication, or erroneously on previous studies of wolf social behavior. Thankfully, you can rest at ease because regardless of your dog's behavior, he is never trying to exert an alpha status or pull rank on any human inside or outside of the home. Individual relationships are learned through experience, rather than motivated by a desire to dominate.[12]

Throughout the past several decades, the study of dog behavior has been based on observations of adult wolf behavior. Misinterpretation of wolf behavior and the application of dominance theory are detrimental to our relationship with dogs because it suggests we maintain a dominant or leadership-based and controlling relationship with our dogs. Humans never have to be the alpha by performing rollovers, scruff shakes, holding their dogs mouth shut, or any other punishment-based techniques recommended to maintain rank. Confrontational training methods, whether staring down dogs, striking them, or intimidating them with physical manipulation does little to correct improper behavior and can elicit aggressive responses.[13]

When a person forces his dog into a submissive posture by rolling the dog on his side, the person is actually being confrontational and aggressive to the dog. These techniques often result in human injury and elicit a fear response in the dog. In a wolf pack, a lower-ranking wolf will voluntarily offer a submissive posture in order to appease and avoid confrontation. This is a ritualized behavior of wolves that cannot be mimicked or duplicated through human-dog interactions. More understanding of the social system of the domestic dog will come from evaluating dogs in the human domestic environment rather than making comparisons with wolves. Similarly, although comparisons can be made, we cannot fully understand the social construct of human behavior by evaluating the behavior of chimpanzees.

**Key points:**

- Dogs do not share dominance hierarchies with people; there is no need to maintain a dominant- or leadership-based relationship with our dogs.

- Dominance techniques are dangerous and damaging to the human-dog bond.

## The Senses

In order to understand social behavior and communication, we need to evaluate how dogs perceive the world. Your dog's senses affect how he learns and how he communicates with people and other dogs. Methods of communication include visual (body language), vocal (sound), and scent (smells). Dogs interpret a message by evaluating multiple communication signals simultaneously. Knowing how dogs perceive their surroundings and communicate allows us to have a clearer and more satisfying relationship with them.

### *Sight*

Dogs have color vision, but their vision is of a limited color spectrum when compared to people. Canine vision is comparable to a person who is red and green colorblind. Dogs see blue-violet, yellow-green, and shades of gray. The colors blue and yellow are very distinct to dogs. Dogs have a wider field of view when compared to people (dogs: 245 degrees; humans: 180 degrees). This makes dogs better able to see objects in their peripheral vision. Binocular vision overlaps 30 to 60 degrees in dogs compared to 140 degrees in people. The field of depth perception is more limited in dogs. Field of vision and the binocular component will vary slightly based on breed conformation (eye set), and selection for working ability (greyhound vs. bulldog). Vision is best at close proximity. Object movement is important for detection at greater distances. Dogs can also see well in dim light. The visual acuity (resolution) of most dogs is relatively poor (20/75) compared to most humans (20/20). Seeing eye service dogs, through selective breeding, have an acuity closer to 20/20. Similar to people, visual acuity may decline with age.

**Key points:**

- Your dog's senses affect how he learns and communicates.

- Canine vision is comparable to a person who is red and green colorblind.

- The visual acuity of most dogs is relatively poor (20/75) compared to most humans (20/20).

## Hearing

Dogs have an incredible sense of hearing and are better able to hear high frequencies than people. The hearing ability of dogs will vary based on breed and age. Research conducted by George M. Strain indicates the frequency range of dogs is greater than that of humans (dogs: 67–45,000 Hz; humans: 64–23,000 Hz). Dogs, like people, hear best at about 4,000 Hz. Dogs have an exceptional ability to localize the source of a sound by moving their ears and by comparing the time delay between ears. Your dog may even tilt his head to one side when listening. In terms of the message communicated, sounds of high tonal pitch tend to be distance-decreasing sounds (come closer) compared to sounds of low tonal pitch which are distance increasing (go away). A whimper, whine, or howl has a high tonal pitch and different meaning from a low-pitch grunt or growl. The sensitivity of a dog's ears makes it unnecessary to shout when training. If you want your dog to come to you, use a high-pitch voice instead of a stern, deep voice. The meaning of barking will vary based on the context or social situation. Understanding how dogs hear and the meaning of vocalizations allows us to better communicate with them.

## Smell

A dog's nose has approximately 250 million receptor cells compared to about 5 million in people. The surface area lining the canine nose consists of 20–200 square centimeters compared to 2 to 4 square centimeters in people. A dog's sense of smell is 1 to 100 million times better than people at detecting butyric acid (chemical found in human sweat). Dogs have demonstrated the ability to detect a human fingerprint on a pane of glass after 1 month duration. For these reasons, dogs excel at tracking, trailing, and scent detection. A dog's sense of smell may be its most powerful and important sense. Dogs are able to recognize people and other dogs simply by the way they smell. Your dog can smell you across the room; it is not necessary to reach for him or have strangers put their hand under his nose. Dogs will sniff the ground in order to obtain information about who was there (human, dog, or prey). It can be great mental stimulation to allow your dog to smell things when out for a walk. Pheromones are chemical messages found in urine, stool, anal sac secretions, and glandular secretions. These chemical messages are used in everyday communication between dogs. Glandular secretions are derived from the head, feet, base of the tail, anus, and sexual organs.

## Taste

Taste in dogs is similar to that of people. Dogs are most sensitive to sweets. They prefer novel foods and enjoy fatty foods. Bitter or sour tastes are likely to be avoided. Palatability of food is affected by texture, smell, temperature, and taste. Many studies suggest dogs prefer cooked meat compared to raw. Preferences or aversions may be established early in life.

**Key points:**

- The hearing frequency range of dogs is greater than that of humans.

- If you want your dog to come to you, use a high-pitch tone of voice.

- A dog's sense of smell is 1 to 100 million times better than people's at detecting a chemical found in human sweat.

- It can be great mental stimulation to allow your dog to smell things when out for a walk.

- Similar to people, dogs prefer novel, sweet, and fatty foods.

### *Touch*

Touch receptors are located at the base of every hair and especially at the vibrissa (whiskers). Similar to people, the skin of dogs is able to detect pain, pressure, chemical stimulation, and temperature. Your dog's coat will affect his sensitivity to temperature extremes. Dogs can only lose heat by panting or perspiring through their feet. Dogs are unable to regulate their body temperature as efficiently as people.

Physical contact is important for relationships and maintaining the social bond. Touch calms, and reduces heart rate and stress levels. Dogs tend to prefer deep muscle massage and long firm strokes from their head to hindquarters. Most dogs are not fond of being hugged. Many dogs are sensitive to touch on areas surrounding their nose, mouth, feet, flanks, and tail. Your dog may have individual preferences or aversions for being touched, similar to people.

## Communication

Dogs communicate mainly by using body language. Signaling is accomplished by positioning the head (mouth, eyes, and ears), body, and tail. Variation amongst different dog breeds and the morphology or lack of these appendages can lead to miscommunication amongst dogs and humans. Humans are verbally oriented and not as aware of body language. Dogs are better at social cognition (the ability to detect subtle social cues in humans) than wolves or chimpanzees.[14] Because dogs are very good at reading our body language, they can often predict our behavior even if we think we have not given any behavioral indication. Humans, on the other hand, are not very good at reading dogs' body language. There is much miscommunication between dogs and people. We do not understand each others language!

### *Conflict/Appeasement Behaviors*

Conflict or appeasement behaviors were first referred to as "calming signals."[15] They are normal behaviors used to communicate appeasement or uneasiness and some are ritualized amongst dogs. Ritualized conflict behaviors are understood between the sender and receiver and are used in canine communication. Conflict behaviors may occur on a conscious or subconscious level. When these behaviors are displayed in specific contexts, they mean your dog is uneasy with the social interaction or situation. However, humans often do not pick up on some of these subtle cues. See Table 2.1 for a list of common conflict/appeasement behaviors

**Key points:**

- Dogs are unable to regulate their body temperature as well as people, and can only lose heat by panting or perspiring through their feet.

- Touch calms, reduces heart rate and stress levels, and is important for maintaining social relationships.

- Dog mainly communicate through body language.

- Conflict or appeasement behaviors indicate uneasiness with a situation and are a prelude to social tension and aggression.

## TABLE 2.1: CONFLICT/APPEASEMENT BEHAVIORS

| | |
|---|---|
| Yawning | Scratching |
| Licking lips/nose | Belly exposure |
| Turning head away | Sniffing the ground |
| Looking away | Curving body into a "C" shape |
| Squinting eyes | Play bow |
| Shifting eyes | Lifting front paw |
| Sneezing | Mounting/humping |
| "Wet dog" shake off | Hackles raised |

Conflict behaviors may be a precursor to aggression:

1. Notice pinned ears and tucked tail (fear and uneasiness)

2. Avoiding eye contact

3. Lip licking

4. Growling and showing teeth (aggression)

(This dog was uncomfortable with the costumes, but it never showed aggression toward the children. This is one of their own dogs, and the showing of the teeth was actually the dog eating a treat.)

Look for these behaviors in your own dog. He may be trying to communicate uneasiness with a situation. Conflict behaviors are used to decrease social tension and aggression in dogs. They are a way of your dog telling you or another dog, "Please back off, you are making me uneasy." In some dogs, they are a precursor to aggression. Many of these behaviors are considered polite communication between dogs. Miscommunication between you and your dog can lead to frustration. For example, while training your dog, you lean over him and command in a stern voice, "Sit!" Consequently your dog does not sit and instead he sniffs the ground and looks away from you. Many owners would misinterpret this as disobedience when actually your dog is trying to communicate that he is uncomfortable with the situation (your threatening tone and stance). Your dog is being polite and communicating to you in his native language. Try to understand your dog's body language and avoid inducing conflict in your dog.

## Characteristics of Dogs

When living with dogs it is important to set realistic expectations. Dogs are dogs, and they are going to do dog things. We are not going to stop dogs from having innate behaviors, nor should we expect them never to perform these intrinsic canine behaviors. Expectations of dogs are often more than we would expect from ourselves or other people. Fortunately, because dogs are intelligent, we can teach dogs and they can learn human-appropriate responses in various contexts. Knowing some general characteristics of dogs helps us understand them better. These dog characteristics are modified from *The Culture Clash* by Jean Donaldson (James and Kenneth Publishers, 1996).

Dogs are amoral. They do not know right from wrong. They know safe and unsafe. For example, it is safe to get into the trash when people are absent but unsafe when they are present.

Dogs are opportunistic and self centered. It is about what's in it for them.

Dogs are social. This is why they make good companions.

Dogs are constantly learning from their actions. Learned behaviors may be appropriate or inappropriate for human counterparts. Let's evaluate their behavior from a learning perspective.

Dogs explore the world with their mouths. They lack thumbs. Everything is a potential chew toy.

By remembering these characteristics, it is easier to explain and understand some unwanted dog behaviors. Rather than forcing relationships based on dominance, we suggest a parenting relationship based on trust, guidance, and teaching our dogs appropriate responses.

## *Successful Canine Parenting*

To be a successful canine parent follow these simple rules:

### Understand a dog's perspective—be fair
Remember dogs are amoral, opportunistic, self-centered, social, constantly learning, and explore the world with their mouths. To be anthropomorphic, dogs make the most of current opportunities because life is short and time is fleeting—Carpe diem.

### Be a good teacher
Control what your dog learns. Guide him into making the right decisions. Set your dog up to succeed. Don't waste your time telling your dog what not to do. Instead, teach him the correct behavior.

### Communicate clearly
Your job is to communicate to your dog when he is performing a correct behavior. Catch him doing appropriate behaviors and reward him for it! A frequent occurrence of positive reinforcement will help your dog learn quickly.

### Be consistent
Inconsistency and unpredictability cause fear and anxiety leading to behavioral problems. Reprimanding jumping one day and rewarding it the next will confuse your dog. Set the rules of the household and make your interactions predictable and consistent.

### Be your dog's advocate
Your dog cannot speak up for himself. Be aware of his body language and protect him from overwhelming situations. A well-meaning group of children running over and surrounding your puppy can be frightening. You need to be willing to intervene and prevent negative experiences.

**Key points:**

- The optimal canine parent is fair, a good teacher, communicates clearly, and consistent with human-dog interactions.
- The principles of canine rearing are very similar to child-rearing; set rules and be your dog's advocate.

The principles of canine-rearing are very similar to child-rearing. Strive to be a fair and consistent canine parent. Provide guidance, direction, consistency, predictability, and security rather than punishment. Undesirable behaviors must have consequences, but the consequence should be designed to create learning rather than fear. Physical and verbal reprimands are unnecessary.

# References

1. Savolainen P, Zhang Y, Luo J, Lundeberg J, and Leitner T. 2002-11-22. Genetic evidence for an East Asian origin of domestic dogs. *Science*, 298 (5598): 1610–3.

2. Miklosi A. *Dog Behaviour, Evolution, and Cognition.* Department of Ethology, Eötvös University, Budapest, Hungary. Oxford University Press, 2007.

3. Mech LD. Alpha status, dominance, and division of labor in wolf packs. *Canadian Journal of Zoology* 77:1196–1203. Jamestown, ND: Northern Prairie Wildlife Research Center Home Page. http://www.npwrc.usgs.gov/resource/2000/alstat/alstat.htm (Version 16MAY2000)

4. Mech LD. Alpha status, dominance, and division of labor in wolf packs. *Canadian Journal of Zoology* 77:1196–1203. Jamestown, ND: Northern Prairie Wildlife Research Center Home Page. http://www.npwrc.usgs.gov/resource/2000/alstat/alstat.htm (Version 16MAY2000)

5. Mech LD. *The Wolf: The Ecology and Behavior of an Endangered Species.* University of Minnesota Press, Minneapolis, 1970 (8th ed. 1995).

6. Semyonova A. The social organization of the domestic dog; a longitudinal study of domestic canine behavior and the ontogeny of domestic canine social systems. 2003, The Carriage House Foundation, The Hague, www.nonlineardogs.com, version 2006.

7. Beck AM. *The Ecology of Stray Dogs: A Study of Free-Ranging Urban Animals.* York Press, Baltimore. 1973 [re-published by Purdue University Press, West Lafayette, IN, 2002]

8. Coppinger R, Coppinger L. *Dogs: A Startling New Understanding of Canine Origin, Behavior and Evolution.* New York: Simon & Schuster, Inc. 2001.

9. Lindsay SR. *Handbook of Applied Dog Behavior and Training. Vol. 1,* Iowa State University Press, Ames, Iowa, 2000, p 20.

10. Pettijohn TF, Wong TW, Ebert PD, and Scott JP. 1977. Alleviation of separation distress in 3 breeds of young dogs. *Dev Psychobiol*, 10:373–381.

11. Rooney NJ, Bradshaw JWS, and Robinson IH. A comparison of dog-dog and dog-human play behaviour. *Applied Animal Behaviour Science*, Volume 66, Issue 3, 29 February 2000, pp 235–248.

12. Bradshaw JWS, Blackwell EJ, Casey RA. Dominance in dogs—useful construct or bad habit? *Journal of Veterinary Behavior: Clinical Applications and Research* (May/June 2009), pp 135–144.

13. Herron MH, Shofer FS, and Reisner IR. Survey of the use and outcome of confrontational and non-confrontational training methods in client-owned dogs showing undesired behaviors. *Applied Animal Behaviour Science*, Volume 117, Issues 1–2, February 2009, pp 47–54.

14. Hare B, Brown M, Williamson C, and Tomasello M. The domestication of social cognition in dogs. *Science*, 22 November 2002: Vol. 298. no. 5598, pp 1634–1636.

15. Rugaas T. 1997. *On Talking Terms with Dogs: Calming Signals.* Hawaii: Legacy By Mail, Inc.

# HOW DOGS LEARN

## How Dogs Learn

Learning is the process that modifies a dog's behavior or knowledge as the result of interaction with the environment. A behavior is acquired, omitted, or changed as the result of experience. The term *conditioning* is synonymous with the term learning.

> *Conditioning*—learning of a response to a stimulus.

Generally, learned behaviors are easy to change or modify, except those learned early in life. Multiple behavioral studies indicate the learning ability of an 8-week-old puppy is equal to that of an adult dog. Puppies should start foundation training at 8 weeks of age. Don't worry! If your dog is an adolescent or even older, he is still capable of learning. Although there are sensitive periods for behavioral acquisition, learning is a continuous process. Even older dogs can learn new tricks.

## Learning and Innate Drive

All behavioral responses are controlled by genetics and modified through learning. Your dog's genetic programming determines his breed-specific behavioral repertoire.

Most breeds of dogs were selectively bred for a specific task. Your dog's heritable working characteristics will vary based on pedigree and individual personality. Examples of breed groups include sporting, hound, working, terrier, and herding. Sporting dogs include pointers, retrievers, setters, and spaniels. They were specifically bred to assist humans with hunting, by manner of pointing and/or retrieving. Hounds were bred for various styles of hunting, using trail scent, sight, or speed to obtain quarry. The roles of working dogs vary in task and may include guarding property, pulling sleds, or working in search and rescue. Terriers were bred to independently hunt and kill vermin. Herding dogs possess the instinctual ability to control the movement of livestock.

There is variability even within breed groups. For example, dogs from the herding group demonstrate herding behavior, yet each breed works livestock via a different style. Herding dogs vary in their use of staring, crouching, and vocalizing. For example, Shetland sheepdogs show a very vocal herding style by barking and actively running and circling livestock, as compared to border collies, who demonstrate a staring, crouching, and stalking style of herding.

**Key points:**

- The learning ability of an 8-week-old puppy is equal to that of an adult dog. This makes 8 weeks of age the ideal time to start foundation training.

- Learning is a continuous process; even older dogs can learn new tricks.

- Genetic programming determines innate breed-specific behavior.

There is breed variability in the predatory behavior of dogs. Terriers tend to be more predatory than other breeds, with most bred to hunt and kill small vermin. Certain components of the predatory sequence are selected for in certain sporting and herding breeds where a specific component of the point, chase, retrieve, and/or bite sequence is desirable. A strong predatory drive may be undesirable when small children or other animals live in the home. Predatory behavior is an innate drive that can be difficult to modify.

Look for breed characteristics to help you determine innate traits your dog may exhibit. Invariably, each dog has his own unique personality based on genetics, learning, and early experience. Don't be surprised if your Sheltie enjoys barking and chasing the kids about the yard, or your beagle seems preoccupied with smelling every blade of grass, or your Jack Russell terrier digs holes in your back yard in search of moles!

## Learning Theory

Dogs learn through classical conditioning and operant conditioning.

### *Classical Conditioning*

Classical conditioning is also known as *Pavlovian* conditioning or associative learning. The scientific study of classical conditioning stems from the work of Ivan Pavlov.

> *Pavlov's Dogs:* Ivan Pavlov experimented with dogs and received a Nobel prize in 1904 for discovering a phenomenon he called a conditioned reflex. While studying the relationship between salivation and digestion, he discovered that stimuli presented to the dogs could induce salivation whether or not food was present. Through repetition, associations were made such that various stimuli (sound, visual, or tactile) became predictive of the presentation of food and thus induced salivation.

Learning through association is a continuous process and it occurs on a conscious or subconscious level. Classical conditioning is a primitive form of learning and it often overrides or actively occurs regardless of the operant response. Involuntary visceral and emotional responses are invoked through classical conditioning.

Classical conditioning has practical applications for dealing with fear and anxiety related behaviors. Using classical conditioning, a previously fearful or aversive situation is paired with something pleasant (food, a jolly routine, or relaxation). A change in the emotional response associated with a situation or stimulus is referred to as counter conditioning. Usually, a fearful emotional state is changed to a positive emotional state by adding something pleasant (food) to the situation.

**Key points:**

- A strong predatory drive may be undesirable when small children or other animals live in the home.
- Your dog's personality will be determined by genetics, learning, and early experience.
- Dogs learn through classical conditioning and operant conditioning.
- Classical conditioning is a primitive form of learning where emotional associations are made to environmental or social stimuli.

*Counter conditioning*—the changing of an emotional response through an association with stimulus/stimuli.

Counter conditioning occurs when an emotional response associated with a stimulus is changed. For example, let's imagine your dog shows a moderate startle response to the buzzing sound of an alarm clock. Your dog hears the sound and leaves the bedroom. If every morning when your alarm clock goes off, you toss a handful of tasty treats on the floor, your dog would be less likely to leave the room. Your dog learns to associate the alarm sound with treats. The negative emotional response is changed to a positive emotional response through association. Counter conditioning has occurred.

Counter conditioning is often incorporated with a behavior modification technique known as desensitization.

*Desensitization*—the process of reducing sensitivity or reactivity toward stimuli through gradual controlled exposure.

Using desensitization, gradual exposure (without fear) is accomplished by controlling the distance and/or intensity of the stimulus. Food treats are paired with low levels of the fear-evoking stimulus for counter conditioning. To desensitize properly, you must be able to identify the stimulus, reproduce the stimulus, control its intensity, and find a non-stressful starting point where the dog is willing to take treats.

Let's apply desensitization to the above example of your dog showing a moderate startle response to the buzzing sound of an alarm clock. Desensitization would be accomplished by setting up training situations and controlling the volume of the alarm. A recording could be made of the buzz and then played at a volume that does not induce a fear reaction. While playing the recording, offer your dog food treats (counter conditioning) and gradually increase the volume (without inducing fear). Alternatively, start at a distance from the alarm clock in which your dog is not afraid and gradually decrease the distance (desensitization). The negative emotional response is changed to a positive emotional response through gradual exposure to the full strength stimulus. Counter conditioning and desensitization have occurred.

**Key points:**

- Counter conditioning refers to changing emotional associations and can be beneficial when addressing fearful behavior.

- Desensitization, a behavior modification technique, is often used with counter conditioning.

- Desensitization is the process of reducing sensitivity or reactivity toward stimuli through gradual controlled exposure.

## Operant Conditioning

The scientific study of operant conditioning dates from the beginning of the twentieth century in 1911 with the work of Edward L. Thorndike.

> *Thorndike's Law of Effect:*
>
> - Behaviors that have a pleasant consequence will increase in frequency.
>
> - Behaviors that have an unpleasant consequence will decrease in frequency.

Operant conditioning is also known as *instrumental* learning. With operant conditioning, the result of a behavior influences the likelihood of the behavior occurring again. Hence, the consequence of the behavior is important. If a behavior increases in frequency it has been reinforced. If a behavior decreases in frequency it has been punished. Reinforcement and punishment can be further broken down into positive (adding something) and negative (taking something away).

> *Positive punishment*—the adding of something aversive to decrease a behavior.
>
> *Positive reinforcement*—the adding of something desired to increase a behavior.
>
> *Negative punishment*—the removal of something desired to decrease a behavior.
>
> *Negative reinforcement*—the removal of something aversive to increase a behavior.

**Key points:**

- In operant conditioning, reinforcement increases the likelihood of the behavior occurring again, whereas punishment decreases the likelihood of the behavior occurring again.
- Positive reinforcement occurs when a behavior increases in frequency due to the acquisition of a reward.
- Positive reinforcement should be the primary method of interaction with your dog.

Positive reinforcement should be the primary method of interaction with your dog. Unfortunately, it is human nature to focus on stopping unwanted behavior rather than rewarding desirable ones. Positive reinforcement is underused in most canine households. It should be used often to teach and reinforce appropriate behavioral responses.

Positive reinforcement occurs when a behavior increases in frequency due to the acquisition of a reward. For example, maybe you would prefer your dog not to get on furniture. You observe your dog resting in his dog bed next to the couch. You enter the room and toss a treat to your dog in his bed. Your dog learns that resting in his bed is reinforced by the provision of food. With repetition, your dog will run to his bed in anticipation of a food reward when you enter the room. Your dog will rest in his dog bed rather than on your couch. Resting in his bed will increase in frequency because it has been positively reinforced.

Negative punishment should be the second method of interaction with your dog. There are times when your dog is seeking attention and ignoring him (loss of attention) would be considered a punishment. Negative punishment is preferable to other harsher methods.

Negative punishment occurs when a behavior decreases in frequency due to the removal of something rewarding. For example, maybe you would prefer your dog not to bother you when working at the computer. Your dog nudges you with his nose and paws at you repeatedly. This behavior is attention seeking. In the past, you would talk to him or push him away. If every time your dog performs the behavior you were to ignore him, your dog would learn that nudging and pawing does not get your attention. The behaviors would decrease in frequency and become extinct. Ignoring means not looking at, talking to, or petting him. The removal of attention is a punishment. The behavior is negatively punished.

Positive reinforcement and negative punishment are ethically appropriate methods for dealing with any unwanted behavior.

## Types of Punishment

By definition, there are two types of punishment.

*Positive punishment*—a behavior is given an aversive response and the behavior decreases in frequency.

*Negative punishment*—a behavior results in termination of a pleasant stimulus that is already present and the behavior decreases in frequency.

Methods of punishment delivery include:

*Interactive*—delivered by a person or handler

*Remote*—delivered from a distance (ideally, no handler association)

*Social*—result in abandonment or the handler leaving the dog

## Criteria for Effective Punishment

In order for punishment to be used effectively, 4 criteria must be met.

1. Punishment must be delivered immediately (within half a second of the undesirable behavior).

2. Punishment must occur every time the unwanted behavior occurs.

3. Punishment, by definition, must be of a sufficient intensity to stop the behavior.

4. Punishment should not be associated with the owner or handler of the dog.

Punishment is difficult to apply consistently and is inappropriate in most situations. When one cannot meet the criteria for effective use, punishment becomes abuse.

Positive punishment does not teach your dog what to do, focuses on bad behavior, and does not appease your dog's underlying motivation for the behavior.

**Key points:**

- Negative punishment occurs when a behavior decreases in frequency due removal of something rewarding.

- Positive reinforcement and negative punishment are ethically appropriate methods for dealing with any unwanted behavior.

- Punishment is difficult to apply consistently and is inappropriate in most situations. When one cannot meet the criteria for effective use, punishment becomes abuse.

- Positive punishment does not teach your dog what to do, focuses on bad behavior, and does not appease your dog's underlying motivation for the behavior.

Interactive punishment: Scolding Iris induces fear and withdrawn behavior, and inhibits learning.

## Positive Punishment: It's Not for Your Dog

Although positive punishment can be used to inhibit behavior, it is riddled with problems, and therefore, it's not for your dog.

- Positive punishment is damaging to the human-animal bond.

- Positive punishment inhibits learning and may induce learned helplessness.

- Positive punishment induces anxiety, fear of the handler, or of the environmental situation. One cannot control the dog's perceived association that is going to be made when punishment is applied.

- Positive punishment induces aggression towards humans and dogs.

- Positive punishment does not change the motivation for the behavior.

Verbal or physical reprimands are often used as positive punishment. Shouting "No" or "Ahh" has a negative association, is positive punishment, or a predictor of positive punishment. Telling your dog "No" does not tell him *what to do*. "No" is a vague concept. It may suppress behavior, but it does not teach or tell your dog to perform an appropriate behavior in any given situation. Punishment-based training collars such as pinch collars, choke chains, and electric collars are aversive and meant to induce pain. These examples of verbal and physical punishment are not for your dog! Positive punishment may lead to the development of fear, anxiety, and/or aggressive behavior.

Fortunately, there are ways to reach your goal of training your dog without positive punishment. Remember, positive punishment is inappropriate for puppies and dogs with behavior problems. Positive punishment should not be used to teach new behaviors. Positive punishment does not appease your dogs underlying motivation.

## Stimulus Control

*Generalization* occurs when a dog shows a conditioned reaction to a particular stimulus in a variety of contexts. Dogs do not generalize well. What this means is that learning is place or context specific. When you begin training a new behavior, your dog will likely perform it best in the place he first learned it. Maybe he will "sit" in the kitchen but not out on a walk or at the pet store. A cue is usually a verbal or visual signal that tells your dog to perform a learned behavior. A cue is generalized when your dog will respond reliably in a variety of environments with a variety of distractions.

In order to help your dog generalize a cue, train the behavior in at least 10 different environments. You may need to re-teach the behavior in each new environment. The more places you practice the faster the learning will progress. By training in many environments, your dog will generalize the cue. Behaviors must be taught in various contents or situations with distractions before the behavior is truly known.

*Discrimination* occurs when your dog learns not to respond to a cue which is similar to a previously learned cue. Through training, your dog will learn not to respond unless a cue is given. Your dog will learn to understand the meaning of and to respond to specific cues.

*Overshadowing* and *blocking* occur when two cues are presented simultaneously. When teaching your dog to sit, if you give a visual cue (hand movement upward) and a verbal cue ("sit") at the same time, your dog will only learn the visual cue. Body language is more salient to dogs. The visual cue will overshadow the verbal cue. The verbal cue "sit" will be blocked. Overshadowing and blocking occur because the dog only learns one cue. In order to prevent overshadowing and blocking when teaching a verbal cue, the verbal cue should precede the visual prompt. They should not be given at the same time.

> A cue is under stimulus control when in a training session:
>
> 1.  The dog only offers the behavior in response to the cue (at least 80% of the time).
>
> 2.  The dog does not offer the behavior in response to another different cue.
>
> 3.  The dog does not offer a different behavior in response to the cue.

For example, in a training session, the dog only sits when cued to sit. The dog does not sit when it is cued to lie down. The dog does not lie down when cued to sit. Therefore, the "sit" cue is under stimulus control.

**Key points:**

- When teaching a verbal cue, the verbal cue should precede the visual prompt in order to avoid over-shadowing and blocking.

The cue is under stimulus control when during a training session Sage sits only when cued.

# CHAPTER 4

# SOCIALIZATION

## Socialization

Behavior problems are the greatest threat to the human-animal bond.[1] In fact, behavior problems are the number-one reason why dogs are relinquished to shelters.[2] A bad experience or lack of experience during the first 4 months of a puppy's life can lead to difficult behavior problems, including fear, anxiety, and aggression. The good news is that the Puppy Start Right program will help prevent future problems and allow your puppy to reach his full potential.

> *Lack of experience during the socialization period is just as detrimental as a bad experience.*

To help puppies become comfortable, confident, and emotionally stable adult dogs, they must be properly socialized before 16 weeks of age. After 16 weeks of age, this golden period for social and emotional development has ended, making it difficult for dogs to adapt to the ever-changing world. Many future behavior problems can be prevented through proper socialization, including: 1) aggression to dogs and people; 2) fear of people, places and things; 3) anxiety-related problems; 4) nuisance behaviors such as jumping, chewing, stealing objects, and excessive barking.

If the opportunity to shape a puppy's behavior during the first 4 months of his life is missed, the puppy is more likely to exhibit behavior disturbances later in life and may never reach his full potential. Physical and emotional stability and learning are enhanced through positive exposure to novel experiences during early development.

Just as puppies are vaccinated against infectious diseases during their monthly veterinary visits, they also need to be "vaccinated" against behavior problems. This can be accomplished by enrolling all 7- to 12-week-old puppies in a good puppy socialization class.

> *American Veterinary Society of Animal Behavior's position statement on socialization:* During this time puppies should be exposed to as many new people, animals, stimuli and environments as can be achieved safely and without causing over-stimulation manifested as excessive fear, withdrawal or avoidance behavior.

**Key points:**

- Puppies must be properly socialized before 16 weeks of age.
- Puppies can be "vaccinated" against behavior problems by enrolling them in a good puppy socialization class.
- Lack of exposure during the socialization period can be just as detrimental as a bad experience.

## Socialization Period (3 to 12 weeks of age) < 16 weeks

Dogs experience critical periods of development as they mature. Of particular importance is the socialization period which occurs from 3 to 12 weeks of age. There is some fluidity of the period, but the optimal time for socialization is up to about 12 weeks of age. Between 12 weeks of age and 16 weeks of age, puppies become progressively more reluctant to approach novelty without fear responses. During the socialization period, through repeated and positive exposure to novelty, dogs learn to communicate with humans and other animals and to adapt to a variety of environments.

The socialization period is the most influential learning period of a dog's life. It sets the foundation for many adult behavioral patterns and problems. What a puppy learns during the socialization period will have a life-long effect on his personality and how he reacts to people, other animals, and environments. This is a well documented stage of development in which puppies can readily learn not to fear new things and to develop appropriate social behavior.

## Primary Socialization

The socialization period is divided into primary and secondary socialization. *Primary socialization* occurs during 3 to 5 weeks of age. This time is associated with kinship recognition and the acquisition of canine communication skills. Your dog is learning to identify his own kind and how to communicate with other dogs. Social interactions with littermates increase during this time. Through social play, puppies learn how to inhibit their bite and practice social communication skills. Puppies identify kinship with the most influential social contact provided. Generally, kinship is associated with dogs. However, if a puppy is raised predominantly with another species (cat, sheep, human) other than dogs, it will identify more strongly with that species later in life. Similarly, when raised with the mother and littermates, puppies show an affinity to socialize with their own breed. Breed recognition is observed when puppies demonstrate a preference to associate with other dogs of their own breed.

Puppies display intense signs of distress when separated from the litter, and have a preference for the odor of the mother and littermates. This begins to dissipate around 7 weeks of age, making it the optimal time for secondary socialization. Many social and emotional deficits are observed in adult dogs who are removed too early from the mother and littermates (prior to 6 weeks of age).[3] Some emotional disorders associated with early weaning include separation anxiety, compulsive disorders, hyperactivity, fear, and dog aggression.[4]

The brain is not fully developed and a traumatic experience during primary socialization is not likely to have a profound impact on future behavior.

**Key points:**

- The socialization period occurs from 3 to 12 weeks of age.

- Puppies become progressively more fearful between 12 to 16 weeks of age with the demarcation of the socialization period.

- The socialization period is the most influential learning period of a dog's life with a lifelong effect on his personality and how he reacts to people, other animals, and environments.

- Primary Socialization, from 3 to 5 weeks of age, is associated with kinship recognition and the acquisition of canine communication skills.

- Many social and emotional deficits are observed in adult dogs who are removed too early from the mother and littermates (prior to 6 weeks of age).

"Prior to 5 weeks, puppies are virtually immune to lasting negative impressions, and readily recover from a fearful social experience without permanent avoidance learning."[5]                                    — *Steven R. Lindsay*

## Secondary Socialization

*Secondary socialization* refers to the time from 6 to 12 weeks of age. During this time, puppies become familiar and comfortable in the human domestic environment. Typically, secondary socialization is associated with the puppy leaving the mother and littermates at 7 weeks (+1 or –1 week) and being integrated into the human household. The ideal time to acquire a new puppy is probably 7 to 8 weeks of age. This allows the puppy to begin to develop necessary dog communication skills and prevents behavior disorders associated with early weaning. When the puppies are 7 weeks of age, the mother loses interest in nursing and milk production decreases. This coincides with an increase in motherly discipline and an increase in social competition or fighting between the puppies.

Puppies are most willing to approach a stranger and investigate novel objects with vigorous tail wagging during secondary socialization.[6] As this developmental period comes to an end, novel stimuli will be more likely to induce fear. This is a natural developmental process that occurs in many species. It is a basic survival mechanism. "If I haven't seen it before, I should be afraid because it might eat me."

Profound fear or marked aggression displayed during secondary socialization is abnormal and suggestive of future behavior problems. A young puppy showing intense and prolonged signs of fear will not "grow out of it."

> **Key points:**
>
> - Generally, secondary socialization begins when the puppy leaves the mother and littermates at 7 weeks (+1 or –1 week) and is integrated into the human household.
> - The ideal time to obtain a puppy is 7 to 8 weeks of age.
> - Puppies are most willing to approach a stranger and investigate novel objects with vigorous tail wagging during secondary socialization.

Your puppy should be offered a treat by all unfamiliar people during secondary socialization. This prevents future fear and aggression towards people. Strive to meet the challenge of one new person every day.

# Fear and the Fear Response

During secondary socialization, puppies experience a *fear period* from 8 to 10 weeks of age. This is a normal developmental stage where the puppy is more likely to be fearful and sensitive to traumatic events. A traumatic learning experience during 8 to 10 weeks of age can have a profound negative impact on the overall behavior wellness of the dog. For example, a single traumatic experience of a bicycle falling near the puppy at 8 weeks of age may predispose the dog to a lifelong fear of bicycles. Puppies should not be shipped during the fear period. Safeguard your 8– to 10-week-old puppy and provide positive learning experiences during the fear period.

A second fear period occurs between 4 and 12 months of age and can last up to 3 weeks.[7] This period is associated with a fear of familiar objects or novel environmental stimuli. Watch for signs of this period and help your puppy through any fearful situations.

Fear is a normal and adaptive behavior of dogs. Don't expect your puppy never to become frightened. More importantly, your puppy should readily recover from novel and mild fear inducing stimuli. At some point your puppy will encounter something that is startling or produces a fear response. How will you know he is afraid? Here are some common signs your puppy is afraid:

- Ears pulled back or down to the side
- Tail tucked
- Hiding
- Freezing
- Shaking
- Pacing, running, or escape behavior
- Seeking close human contact

Piloerection (hair standing erect over the shoulders and back) is a sign of high arousal, fear, and uncertainty. Urination, defecation, and anal gland expression are more profound signs of fear or panic. When dogs are afraid, there may be a fight or flight response. Most of us recognize the above signs of fear; however some puppies may show more aggressive signs when afraid or threatened. Aggression may include barking, growling, snapping, and/or biting. These behaviors, delivered in a threatening manner when frightened, are not normal behavioral responses for puppies in their socialization period. Aggression should be evaluated by a qualified animal behavior professional immediately. (See Appendix for a listing of qualified animal behavior professionals.)

A puppy less than 3 months of age should readily recover and not remain in a heightened state of fear or anxiety when exposed to novelty. Proper socialization involves positive exposure to novelty, and allow the puppy to investigate and overcome any apprehension associated with environmental stimuli.

**Key points:**

- The first fear period, between 8 to 10 weeks of age, is a normal developmental stage when puppies are more likely to be fearful and sensitive to traumatic events.

- Puppies should not be shipped during the first fear period.

- A second fear period may occur during adolescence.

- Fear is a normal and adaptive behavior of dogs in certain contexts and situations.

- A puppy less than 3 months of age should readily recover and not remain in a heightened state of fear or anxiety when exposed to novelty.

**1.** Iris is relaxed. Her ears are forward and her body stance is neutral.

**2.** Iris is showing signs of fear; her ears are pinned back, she is leaning away, and she is frozen. Although you cannot see it in the picture, her tail is also tucked.

> **Key points:**
>
> • Avoid comforting or coddling your puppy when he is frightened.
>
> • Fear responses are best dealt with through counter conditioning and desensitization.

### *What should I do when my puppy is frightened?*

How you react to the situation can have a profound impact on your puppy's future response to frightening stimuli. Avoid comforting your puppy with soothing talk or excessive petting. Telling your puppy, "It's OK," can actually make the future fear responses more intense. There are two reasons that coddling your puppy when he is frightened may be problematic:

1. If your puppy is taught to find you when he is frightened, what is he to do if you are not there? A dog that is afraid of thunderstorms and has been conditioned to find his owner during storms may attempt to break out of the house in a panicked effort to find his owner, if his owner is not home when a storm occurs.

2. Although it is human nature to want to comfort your puppy, the change in your behavior may actually reinforce or justify the fear response. The soothing talk to calm your puppy down may become a predictor that something unpleasant is about to happen. Dogs are very sensitive to subtle changes in our behavior and detect when we are worried or nervous. The dog that is trembling and shaking while on the veterinary examination table learns when his owner tells him, "It's OK," unpleasant things are about to happen (injections, rectal temperature, etc.).

Your puppy will likely feel more comfortable if he is able to be near you when in a frightening situation. This is acceptable. Do not shun or push your puppy away. Simply remain calm and nonchalant about the situation, as if nothing unusual is happening.

Avoid correcting or yelling at your puppy. Reprimanding him will not reduce his fear.

When addressing fear reactions and socializing your puppy, you will utilize two behavior modification techniques: counter conditioning and desensitization.

*Counter conditioning*—the process of replacing a negative or neutral emotional response to a stimulus with a positive emotional response.

*Desensitization*—the process of reducing sensitivity or reactivity toward stimuli through gradual controlled exposure.

**Key points:**

- Desensitization and counter conditioning are used proactively during socialization in order to prevent fear responses and facilitate positive learning experiences.

- If your puppy is afraid, offer him special treats to facilitate counter conditioning.

- Allow your puppy to investigate frightening stimuli at his own pace.

- Control your distance from frightening stimuli in order to allow for desensitization.

- Verbal encouragement can potentially condition a fear response; your best bet is to let the treats do the talking.

Counter conditioning and desensitization are often used together for fear responses. These techniques should be used proactively during socialization and exposure. Food treats are paired with a low level of fear-evoking stimuli. Food changes the emotional response from an unpleasant to a pleasant emotion (counter conditioning). Using desensitization, gradual exposure (without fear) is accomplished by controlling distance and intensity of the stimulus. The further your puppy is away from the object, the less frightened he will be. To desensitize properly, you must be able to identify the stimulus, reproduce the stimulus, control its intensity, and find a non-stressful starting point where the puppy is still taking treats. If your puppy suddenly stops taking treats or starts grabbing roughly at the treats, you have progressed too quickly. If desensitization is implemented improperly such that you induce fear of the stimulus, your puppy is likely to become more sensitive or afraid of the stimulus with future encounters.

If your puppy becomes frightened, your first response should be to use treats liberally. Throw a handful of small soft tasty treats on the ground right in front of your puppy. Because of constraints on learning, treats cannot reinforce fear or behaviors associated with fear. For example, suppose you are afraid of cockroaches but every time you see a cockroach your best friend gives you $20 or $100 or even $1000. The money does not make you more afraid of roaches. Actually the opposite happens. You may begin to look forward to seeing a roach... as long as it doesn't get too close! Your heart is less likely to race and you become less reactive to the sight of roaches. In contrast, if your friend held you close and comforted you, although you may calm down, the next time you see a roach you will still be afraid. Your emotional state towards roaches has not changed.

Your puppy should be allowed to investigate any frightening stimulus at his own pace. When your puppy is on leash, avoid pulling him towards the frightening stimulus. Allow your puppy to approach on his own terms. If your puppy is not taking treats or not recovering quickly, you will need to move away from the frightening stimulus. Move a distance away so your puppy is able to relax and take treats. This is your non-stressful starting point.

You may use a "jolly routine" by acting silly and playing with your dog with his favorite toy. The goal is to change his motivational state. This is different than coddling but should be used with caution. The "jolly routine" can be difficult to use effectively and potentially can condition the fear response if done improperly. Your voice may reflect your anxiety and your sudden change in behavior may become a predictor of potential dangers in the environment. Your best bet is to let the treats do the talking.

- Do use treats liberally.

- Do allow the puppy to investigate at his own pace.

- Do get your puppy to a non-stressful starting point.

- Avoid coddling or reprimanding when fearful.

Example #1: Your puppy is on leash and you are walking down the street. The neighbors have placed a For Sale sign in their front yard. You are about 20 feet from the sign when you see your puppy stop in his tracks. He is staring at the sign and leaning slightly backwards and away from it. His tail is slightly tucked and his ears are pinned back against his head. The hair on his shoulders or rump seems raised (piloerection). He let's out a little "woof, woof" and jumps forward towards the sign and then back again. He is afraid. Immediately drop a handful of small treats on the ground and allow him to eat them. If he takes a step closer to the sign give him a treat. You may approach the sign yourself, tossing treats along the way. The leash should remain slack and very little verbal encouragement should be used. You should remain standing upright and let the puppy approach the sign. Your puppy should very quickly relax (tail and ears return to a normal position) and investigate the sign. Give a few more treats then continue on your walk. The next sign that you see, proactively offer your puppy treats.

1. Tossing a handful of small treats on the sidewalk at a distance from the For Sale sign facilitates counter conditioning.

2. Approaching the sign and allowing the dog to approach at his own pace. The leash should be loose. Reward with food treats.

3. Proactively offer treats at the next sign.

Example #2: You are walking your puppy on leash and a garbage truck approaches you. Your puppy tucks his tail and pulls at the end of the leash trying to run away from the truck. You should calmly turn and walk to a distance away from the truck and give your puppy treats. If he is still not taking treats, increase the distance from the truck and offer treats again. Once he is taking treats, continue to give them until the truck has passed. Keeping him focused on you with one treat after another while the truck is passing by will make the truck less scary. Next time, offer your puppy treats as soon as he sees or hears a truck in the distance to continue positive associations with garbage trucks.

Notice Iris' ears pinned with the sound of the truck. This is a fear response. Go to a distance away from the garbage truck and offer lots of small tasty treats for counter conditioning. In the future, offer treats with the sight or sound of garbage trucks in the distance to change your dog's emotional response.

# Puppy Socialization Classes

Puppy socialization classes are a controlled way to expose your puppy to novel people, dogs, and environmental stimuli. In one study, dogs that had not attended puppy socialization classes were more likely to display behavior problems involving fear or aggression towards strangers, unfamiliar dogs or environmental stimuli.[8] All 7–12 week old puppies should be enrolled in a good puppy socialization class. The socialization period is a great time to start foundation training. The brain and learning ability of puppies is adult-like, based on electroencephalogram studies, at 8 weeks of age.[9] Attending puppy socialization classes is the single most important thing you can do for your dog in his lifetime.

## *Importance of Social Play and Training*

Through social play, puppies learn how to communicate and interact with other dogs. Puppies need opportunities to play with other puppies of various breeds in order to develop normal canine communication skills. Puppies play differently with other puppies than they do with adult dogs; similarly, adult dogs play differently with puppies than they do with other adult dogs. Exposure to a variety of different breeds, puppies and adults is important during this time. Dog breeds vary in appearance and have different play styles. Puppies deprived of play during this period may be incapable of play later in life. In addition, poor social skills can contribute to dog aggression.

Foundation training should include teaching your puppy how to play with toys and people. Ball and toy drive may not occur naturally, although for some dog breeds a strong inherited predatory drive exists. Retrieving and play with toys is a learned behavior that must be established at a young age. Dogs that enjoy playing with people and toys are more easily trained. Learning to interact with people in order to receive rewards should be nurtured during the socialization period.

**Key points:**

- All 7–12 week old puppies should be enrolled in a good puppy socialization class.

- Through social play, puppies learn how to communicate and interact with other dogs, play with other puppies, and play with toys and people.

- The socialization period is a great time to start foundation training because the brain and learning ability of puppies is adult like at 8 weeks of age.

## What makes a good puppy class?

A good puppy socialization class limits the age of puppies to the socialization period (less then 16 weeks of age). Proof of initiation of a vaccination series with a veterinary examination at least 10 days prior to class should be required to attend a class. The number of puppies allowed in the class should be limited based on staff ratio and facility size. Classes should be instructed by individuals who are specially trained in animal behavior, learning theory, and canine development, as well as medical conditions and disorders.

A good puppy class does not recommend the use of verbal or physical reprimands including corrective collars such as a pinch, choke, or shock. Interrupters such as, "Ah," "No," or "Wrong" are not used to teach new behaviors or address problem behaviors. Treats should be used liberally.

## The format of a good puppy socialization class includes:

- **Puppy Play Sessions:** Controlled off-leash short play sessions (5 minutes) with other puppies in a secure environment.

- **Sights and Sounds:** Exposure to novel environments, people, objects, surfaces, and sounds in a fun and positive manner.

- **Health and Handling:** Instruction to help you prepare your puppy to accept routine procedures at home, in the veterinary hospital, and/or grooming facility.

- **Puppy Parenting Tips:** Education on normal canine body language, learning, problem solving, and puppy parenting.

- **Basic Puppy Manners:** Training to address common puppy problems such as biting, jumping, chewing, stealing objects, food bowl safety, and house training.

There are numerous classes available for puppies, but most are not "true" socialization classes. Instead, they focus on obedience training of the juvenile (3 to 6 months) or adolescent dog (6 to 18 months). Although training is an important component of a socialization class, the focus should be on positive interactions with numerous dogs, people, and objects. Maximize your puppy's potential by enrolling him in an appropriate puppy socialization class.

**Key points:**

- A good puppy class uses treats liberally and does not recommend the use of verbal or physical reprimands including corrective collars.

- In order to socialize your puppy properly, he will need to be comfortable wearing a collar and leash.

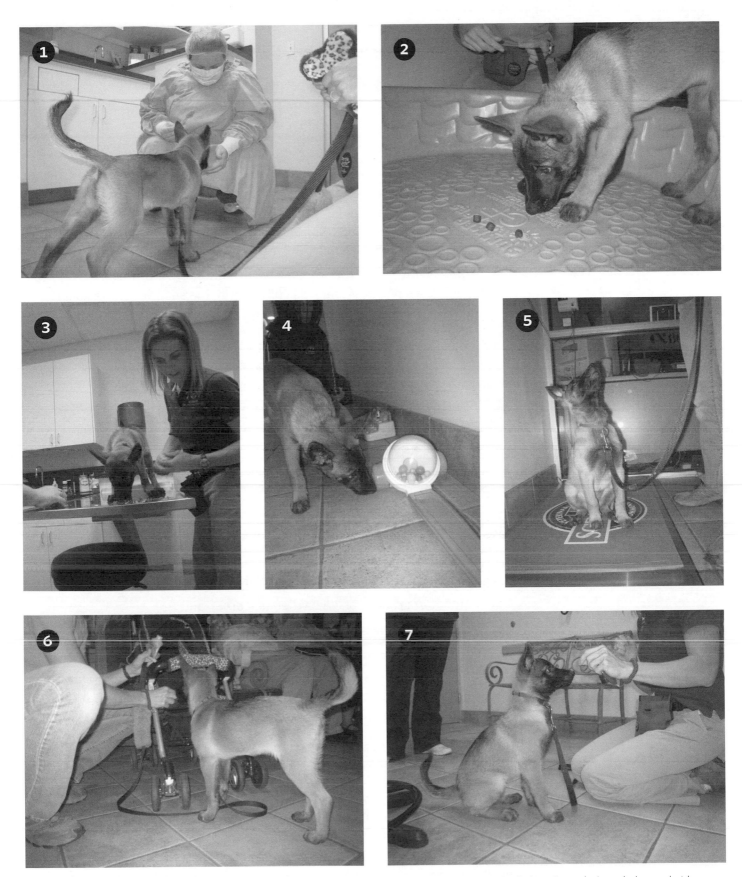

**1.** Jazmin, 10-week-old Belgian Malinois, meeting a technician in surgical attire and receiving treats. **2.** Jazmin exploring a baby pool at her own pace. **3.** Offering treats on the exam table for health and handling. **4.** Exploring children's toys and finding treats. **5.** Sitting on a rubber mat to be weighed on a floor scale. **6.** Taking treats off of a stroller for exposure to objects with wheels. **7.** Teaching basic puppy manners with positive reinforcement.

## Getting Your Puppy Used to a Collar and Leash

In order to socialize your puppy properly, he will need to be comfortable wearing a collar and leash. The socialization period is the perfect time to familiarize your puppy with a collar and leash.

### Collar

The collar should fit snugly around the neck. A nylon or leather non-slip (does not tighten around the neck) collar should be used. You should be able to slip two fingers under it but it should not be able to slip over your puppy's head. You may also consider getting your puppy accustomed to wearing a harness. There are a variety of harnesses available. Since your puppy is growing, check the fit of the collar or harness daily. Every time you attach a leash to your puppy's collar, verify the security of the collar.

Puppies have a variety of reactions to wearing a collar for the first time. They may freeze and act as if unable to walk. Some will scratch at the collar or roll on the ground and try to get it off, while some do not seem to notice. If your puppy reacts negatively to the collar, just ignore him. This is usually short lived. Once he settles down, engage him in play with a toy or give him a few treats.

No matter how your puppy reacts, every time you put on or take off the collar give your puppy a small treat. We want to make a positive rather than just neutral association with being reached for and held by the collar. The collar should be worn the majority of the day while supervised so your puppy becomes accustomed to wearing it. Initially, do not have any tags or accessories attached to the collar.

For safety, remove the collar when your puppy is left alone to prevent accidental strangulation. Take the collar off when your puppy goes in his confinement area and replace it when he comes out.

### Leash

Once your puppy is comfortable with a collar (most puppies adjust within minutes to hours), attach a lightweight 4– to 6-foot leash to your puppy's collar. Similar to putting on or taking off the collar, offer a small treat to your puppy while attaching and detaching the leash.

You may allow your puppy to drag the leash around as you play with him. Never leave a leash attached to your dog unattended because it may get hung up on something or he may eat it.

Pick up the leash and encourage your puppy to follow you by patting your leg and talking sweetly to him. Give him a small treat for coming with you. When he pulls the opposite direction, just stop and wait. The second he turns back toward you, use your marker (see Training section) and reward with a treat. Do not pull, yank or drag your puppy which would induce fear or a negative association with the leash.

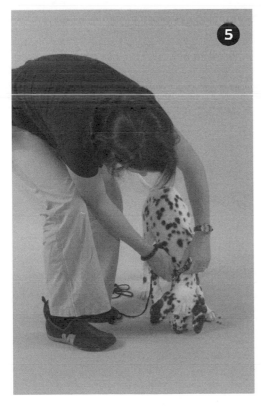

1. Sage is offered canned cheese in preparation of attaching her collar.

2. Attaching the collar while offering canned cheese.

3. Notice the can of cheese between the handler's knees. Sage receives canned cheese while the collar fit is adjusted.

4. More treats are delivered in preparation of attaching the leash.

5. Sage eats treats off the floor while the leash is attached.

6. Sage is encouraged to follow as the handler pats her leg.

# Socialization: Making Exposure Positive

Socialization and exposure are an active and lifelong process. Puppies should be positively exposed to novelty daily during the socialization period. Repeated exposure is important because dogs do not generalize well. Dogs see in "pictures." Learning is situational and context specific. If the "picture" changes in someway, it is new to the dog. So although your puppy may be comfortable meeting new people at the pet store, if he has never met a new person while walking at the park, this is different. Therefore repeated exposure to subtle variations of the same theme is necessary. After the socialization period is over, strive for at least 3 to 4 novel and/or repeated positive experiences a week.

Socialization is not simply about exposure, rather, it is about making exposure fun and positive. This takes planning on your part. Rather than just a neutral experience, make new experiences positive by incorporating treats. Utilize desensitization by gradually exposing your puppy to novelty. Let your puppy acclimate to a new environment by staying clear of the "action" when first arriving. Let your puppy first observe crowds at a distance. Assume your puppy could potentially be afraid of a new person, object, or environment and use treats liberally to prevent a fear response. Be proactive. Control what your puppy learns. Do not wait for the puppy to show signs of fear before initiating treats.

**Key points:**

- Socialization is an active and lifelong process.

- Socialization is not about simple exposure, but making exposure fun and positive with liberal use of treats.

- Do not wait for your puppy to show signs of fear before initiating treats; be proactive.

## Taking it on the road...

- Take a variety of pea-sized, soft, tasty, treats.

- Bring your puppy's favorite toy.

- Your puppy should be hungry.

- Remember water and a bowl, a proper-fitting buckle collar or harness and a 6-foot leash.

- Be aware of your puppy's body language.

- Be your puppy's advocate.

- Be proactive.

- Allow your puppy to explore at his own pace.

- Situations should be controllable. You must be able to manipulate your distance and remove your puppy from the situation if necessary.

- Have fun!

## *Environments*

Expose your puppy to a multitude of environments. Your dog is likely to live at least 10 to 15 years; you cannot always anticipate future moves or lifestyle changes. If you live in a rural or suburban setting, take trips to an urban setting and vice versa. Instead of taking your puppy to the same park every day, try a new park. Take a trip to the veterinary hospital or grooming facility just for fun. While in the car, go through a drive thru or to the bank. Small food treats should be used throughout the exposure sessions.

1. Iliana is exposed to crowds of people at a distance from a busy outdoor cafe.

2. Exposure to nature and recreational vehicles at a state park.

3. Offering treats at a distance from passing crowds in a public square.

4. Iliana is offered treats on the exam table and greeted by a technician during a veterinary clinic fun visit.

## *People*

Strive for your puppy to meet at least one new person a day during his socialization period. Encounters should occur in your home, as well as in different environments. Postal workers and people in uniform approaching your home are important. Meeting a variety of people in an unobtrusive and fun manner helps dogs generalize that new people are nothing to fear.

Puppies should meet people of different ages, sex, and ethnic backgrounds. Children are one of the primary recipients of dog bites. It is important to socialize your puppy with children of various ages. Children should never be left unattended with any dog. Allowing a child to grab or hug your puppy will not be a positive experience. Because your puppy may accidently pinch the child's hand when taking a treat, small children should be encouraged to drop treats on the floor. To a dog, a 3-year-old toddler looks and behaves very differently than a tall man with a beard wearing a baseball hat.

When encountering new people, you should give your puppy several small extra special treats. This will teach your puppy to first look to you when meeting people. Give your puppy a cue, such as "Say hello." Have the person give a treat. Let your puppy spend 15 to 30 seconds with the person. Reward him with a treat or his favorite toy for coming back to you. Initially, it is not necessary for your puppy to sit when meeting unfamiliar people. You will add the sit for greeting after your puppy has had many fun experiences with unfamiliar people and he knows the sit cue reliably.

When exposing your puppy to crowds, it is important to control your distance from the crowd. Crowds can be overwhelming. Stay on the outskirts initially, and then partake in short sessions of walking through the crowd. At each step in the process your puppy should be receiving numerous small treats. During these social experiences, your focus should remain on your puppy at all times.

Children in costumes and seniors with handicaps are important people for your puppy to meet.

**1.** Sport is receiving several small treats from his handler when encountering a new person.

**2.** Use a cue, such as, "Go say hi." The handler gives the police officer several treats.

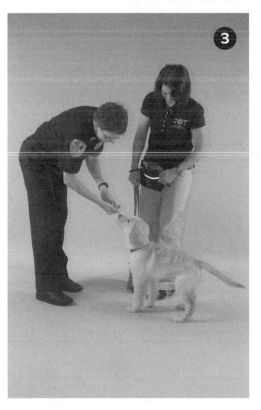

**3.** The police officer gives Sport several treats. It is not necessary for him to sit.

**4.** Sport gets treats for coming back to his handler.

## Animals

Puppies need to have exposure to other animals. A trip to a pet store can help facilitate this process. In a store, it is easier to control your distance from the animals' cages. In a park setting, ducks, geese, birds, squirrels, and rabbits can be frightening or produce high arousal in many dogs. Teach your puppy to focus on you when they encounter these "strange" animals. This will help prevent undesirable arousal problems in the future. At the sight of a squirrel, or other novel animal, use your marker (see Chapter 7: Introduction to Training) and give treats. Keep your puppy focused on you by being animated and upbeat. Pull out his favorite toy. If he is too interested in the novel animal, walk to a distance away or behind a visual barrier and give him treats or play with him.

## Surfaces

Your puppy should encounter grass, gravel, concrete, asphalt, sand, mulch, dirt, metal, plastic, and wood surfaces during the socialization period. Remember to be proactive and reward with treats to make these experiences positive from the start. Tossing several treats on the surface encourages your puppy to explore at his own pace. Some surfaces may be slightly uncomfortable on your puppy's paws. Make exposure to uncomfortable surfaces short and use your puppy's favorite treats. Use caution with surfaces that have openings (drainage grating, wood decks) because your puppy's legs may be small enough to fall through a slat and cause injury.

## Sounds

There are commercially available compact discs (CD) designed to expose puppies to a variety of sounds, including thunderstorms, fireworks, gun shots, children playing, household items, traffic, etc. Using a CD can be helpful because you are able to control the volume and incorporate desensitization. During the socialization period, strive to play a sound CD for your puppy every day while you are home. It may be during meal times or playtimes. Begin with the CD on a low volume at the start of each session. The goal is that your puppy is never frightened by the sounds. Watch for any signs of fear and adjust the volume if necessary. If your puppy is having fun and is not fazed by the sounds, gradually increase the volume throughout the session. Return to a low volume for the start of the next session. Dogs, if not exposed to sounds when young, may become frightened or overwhelmed by everyday sounds. The sound of thunder or a bus or car passing by can be frightening if your puppy is not properly exposed.

## Novelty

Puppies need to have exposure to novelty. Your puppy should have 2 to 3 novel experiences daily during the socialization period and several times a week thereafter. Various items your puppy should encounter include: boxes, bikes, cars, strollers, children's toys, umbrellas, ironing boards, vacuum cleaners, brooms, winter or summer apparel and accessories. The sky is the limit, be creative. A list of suggested socialization experiences are provided at the end of this chapter.

## Potentially Dangerous Situations

There are some environmental situations that should be avoided due to risk of injury. Dangerous situations may arise when and where you least expect them. Roaming dogs or cats may pose a physical threat to your puppy. Picking up your puppy risks conditioning or exacerbating a fear response. Although you should avoid picking your puppy up when frightened, for safety there will be times when you need to carry your puppy. Remain calm, pick your puppy up, and offer treats as you slowly walk away from the situation. Whenever possible, avoid negative and potentially dangerous situations in which your puppy must be removed by carrying him. It is important that you control your puppy's learning experiences and keep them positive.

## Health Risks

Risk of illness from exposure to infectious disease is a concern because puppies have usually not completed their full series of vaccinations until after 16 weeks of age. However, lac k of socialization in public places is behaviorally damaging and of greater risk to your puppy. Vaccines available today provide better protection than those of the past. Vaccinations and early puppy socialization programs are equally important. Early puppy socialization is a way to prevent the development of behavior problems that can eventually result in a failed bond between people and their pets.[10] Millions of dogs die each year due to behavior problems that could have been prevented with proper socialization, far greater than the number the cases due to infectious disease.

Use common sense and minimize your puppy's exposure to infectious disease. Avoid public areas where stray or unvaccinated dogs roam. Know the health and vaccine status of dogs your puppy meets. Keep your puppy's vaccines current and avoid interactions with unvaccinated puppies. Your puppy will require a series of vaccinations, usually given at 3 to 4 week intervals. Check with your veterinary hospital regarding their recommended vaccine protocols and see your veterinarian regularly. Routine fecal examinations and de-worming should be performed by your veterinarian.

Many diseases are passed via contact with feces from an infected dog. When visiting public areas with a very young puppy, restrict your puppy's contact to concrete or asphalt surfaces. This reduces the chance of exposure to infectious disease because grass is a preferred elimination area. Wait 10 days after the first veterinary administered distemper-parvo combination vaccination before implementing intense public exposure. Avoid high traffic dog areas, such as dog parks and dog festivals, until after the second veterinarian-administered distemper-parvo vaccine.

**Key points:**

- Avoid negative and potentially dangerous situations with unfamiliar animals; in doing so, you are controlling your puppy's learning experiences.

- Millions of dogs die each year due to behavior problems that could have been prevented with proper socialization, far greater than the number the cases of infectious disease.

- Minimize your puppy's exposure to infectious disease through routine vaccinations and using common sense.

Exposure and play with other puppies is very important, but know their health status. Look for eye or nasal discharge which may indicate a respiratory infection. Patchy hair loss may indicate external parasites such as mange or mites. Only expose your puppy to other puppies that have been vaccinated by a veterinarian at least 10 days prior. Ten days is the incubation period for parvovirus, a serious infection that causes vomiting and diarrhea and is sometimes fatal. The unfamiliar puppy could be infectious before clinical signs of the illness are exhibited. Before allowing your puppy to interact with another dog, ask the owner how long they have owned the dog, the health and vaccination status of the dog, and whether the dog has had any loose stools in the past 10 days.

Just as children can pass colds to one another, so can puppies pass on infections to each other. Common sense can minimize the chances of infectious encounters. Controlled socialization and exposure is important prior to 3 months of age. The socialization period is a finite period of development only lasting a few months compared to years in humans. Can you imagine how our children would behave if we never let them leave the house or interact with other kids until they were 7 years old?

## References

1.  Houpt KA, Honig SU, Reisner IR. Breaking the human-companion animal bond. *J Am Vet Med Assoc* 1996;208(10):1653–9.

2.  Miller DM, Stats SR, Partlo BS, et al. Factors associated with the decision to surrender a pet to an animal shelter. *J Am Vet Med Assoc* 1996;209:738–742.

3.  Lindsay SR. 2000. *Handbook of Applied Dog Behavior and Training, Volume 1, First Edition.* Iowa State University Press. pp 43–44.

4.  Lindsay SR. 2000. *Handbook of Applied Dog Behavior and Training, Volume 1, First Edition.* Iowa State University Press. pp 43–44.

5.  Lindsay SR. 2000. *Handbook of Applied Dog Behavior and Training, Volume 1, First Edition.* Iowa State University Press. p 46.

6.  Lindsay SR. 2000. *Handbook of Applied Dog Behavior and Training, Volume 1, First Edition.* Iowa State University Press. p 47.

7.  Fox MW. 1978. Socialization patterns in wild and domesticated canids (ch.8), Stages and periods in development: environmental influences and domestication (ch.9), in *The Dog; Its Domestication and Behavior*, New York & London: Garland STPM Press, pp 141–152, 153–176.

8.  Martin ST. Is there a correlation between puppy socialization classes and owner-perceived frequency of behaviour problems in dogs? Masters Thesis, University of Guelph, 2001.

9.  Lindsay SR. 2000. *Handbook of Applied Dog Behavior and Training, Volume 1, First Edition.* Iowa State University Press. p 63.

10. Zawistowski S. Impact of early training on successful pet ownership. The North American Veterinary Conference—2005 Proceedings, p 450.

# PUPPY START RIGHT

## Environments

- ☐ Veterinary Clinic
- ☐ Training Facility
- ☐ Kennel
- ☐ Groomer
- ☐ Pet Store
- ☐ Shopping Mall
- ☐ Work/Office
- ☐ Friend/Relative's House
- ☐ Park/Playground
- ☐ Campground
- ☐ Hotel
- ☐ Airport/Train Station
- ☐ Sporting Events
- ☐ Downtown Intersection
- ☐ Suburbs
- ☐ Rural Areas

### Vehicles
- ☐ Car
- ☐ Bus
- ☐ Boat
- ☐ Train
- ☐ Plane
- ☐ Tractor
- ☐ Motorbike
- ☐ Street Car/Trolley
- ☐ Garbage Truck

### Buildings
- ☐ Stairwells
- ☐ Elevators
- ☐ Elevated Walkway
- ☐ Parking Garage

## Animals

### Dogs and Cats
- ☐ Puppies & Friendly Adult Dogs
- ☐ Kittens & Friendly Adult Cats

### Birds
- ☐ Parrots
- ☐ Ducks and Geese

### Pocket Pets
- ☐ Rodents
- ☐ Rabbits
- ☐ Guinea Pigs
- ☐ Ferrets
- ☐ Reptiles (Snakes, Turtles)

### Farm Animals
- ☐ Horses
- ☐ Livestock

Your puppy should be on leash and wear a well-fitted buckle collar for safety.

Plan ahead and use common sense in order to avoid potentially dangerous situations.

Controlled social experiences and exposure maximizes your puppy's confidence.

Please read the socialization chapter before starting the checklist.

## People

### Age
- ☐ Infants
- ☐ Toddlers
- ☐ Children
- ☐ Teenagers
- ☐ Adults
- ☐ Seniors

### Sex
- ☐ Male
- ☐ Female

### Ethnicity
- ☐ European
- ☐ African
- ☐ Middle Eastern
- ☐ Oriental
- ☐ Asian

### In Uniform
- ☐ Veterinarian
- ☐ Technician
- ☐ Police
- ☐ Security Guard
- ☐ Firefighter
- ☐ Mail Courier
- ☐ Football/Baseball

### Movement
- ☐ Limp
- ☐ Cane
- ☐ Crutches
- ☐ Walker
- ☐ Wheelchair
- ☐ Jogger
- ☐ Biker

### Appearance
- ☐ Tall/Short
- ☐ Thin/Heavy
- ☐ Varied Hair Styles
- ☐ Facial Hair
- ☐ Sunglasses
- ☐ Hats
- ☐ Masks
- ☐ Gloves
- ☐ Costumes
- ☐ Rain Coats
- ☐ Winter Coats
- ☐ Boots

### Smells
- ☐ Perfumes
- ☐ Smoker
- ☐ Alcohol

# SOCIALIZATION CHECKLIST

## Surfaces

- [ ] Rough
- [ ] Slick
- [ ] Wet
- [ ] Dry
- [ ] Cold
- [ ] Warm
- [ ] Wobbly or Unsteady

### Outdoors

- [ ] Sand
- [ ] Mud
- [ ] Soil
- [ ] Grass
- [ ] Gravel
- [ ] Concrete
- [ ] Asphalt
- [ ] Water Puddles
- [ ] Snow
- [ ] Ice
- [ ] Metal Grating

### Indoors

- [ ] Carpet
- [ ] Wood
- [ ] Ceramic
- [ ] Rubber
- [ ] AstroTurf
- [ ] Stairs (Open & Closed)

## Sounds

### Weather

- [ ] Rain
- [ ] Hail/Sleet
- [ ] Wind
- [ ] Thunderstorms

### Environmental

- [ ] Vehicular Traffic
- [ ] Construction Noise
- [ ] Loud Music (Bass/Treble)
- [ ] PA System
- [ ] Whistle
- [ ] Children Playing
- [ ] Screaming/Yelling
- [ ] Gunshots
- [ ] Fireworks

### Household

- [ ] Phone
- [ ] Alarm Clock
- [ ] Doorbell
- [ ] Washer/Dryer
- [ ] Shower
- [ ] Hair Dryer
- [ ] Kitchen Appliances

## Novelty

### Household Items

- [ ] Vacuum
- [ ] Broom
- [ ] Mop
- [ ] Pots and Pans
- [ ] Trash Bags
- [ ] Trash Cans
- [ ] Boxes
- [ ] Luggage
- [ ] Ironing Board
- [ ] Umbrella
- [ ] Children's Toys
- [ ] Baby Carrier
- [ ] Baby Stroller
- [ ] Wagon

### Yard/Garage Equipment

- [ ] Mower
- [ ] Blower
- [ ] Weed Eater
- [ ] Rake
- [ ] Shovel
- [ ] Wheel Barrow
- [ ] Garden Hose
- [ ] Sprinkler
- [ ] Lawn Furniture
- [ ] Power Tools
- [ ] Bicycle
- [ ] Skateboard
- [ ] Rollerblades
- [ ] Kayak/Canoe
- [ ] Skis
- [ ] Surfboards
- [ ] Ladder

- Socialization is not about simple exposure, but making exposure fun and positive with liberal use of treats.

- Your ultimate goal is for your puppy to have positive learning experiences with a variety of stimuli.

- Avoid traumatic experiences and expose your puppy at a safe and comfortable distance that does not elicit fear.

- Do not wait for your puppy to show signs of fear before initiating treats; be proactive.

# CHAPTER 5

# PROBLEM SOLVING & PREVENTION

## Prevention and Management

Prevention exercises and management are important to control what your puppy learns and prevent him from learning undesirable behaviors. The prevention of behavior problems is much easier than the treatment of behavior problems. Your puppy will have natural tendencies and instinctual drives based on his breed. Many behaviors that are problematic to humans are fully acceptable and appropriate in the dog world. Through patience, guidance, and support, you can teach your puppy what is appropriate and acceptable in the human domestic environment and prevent him from making the wrong decisions.

Puppy parents should first realize that even with the most detailed management plan in place, accidents and mistakes will happen. House training will not occur overnight, and something is likely to become chewed. Many of these mistakes are no fault of your puppy, rather they are due to your failure to control the environment and set up your puppy to succeed. Your puppy will do what comes naturally, possibly exploring the world with his mouth. Puppies are opportunistic and do not know the difference between a toy that came from the pet store and a pair of expensive designer shoes.

Just as you would not leave a toddler unsupervised to explore the house, you cannot leave your puppy, either. Begin by puppy proofing the house through the use of baby gates, exercise pens, and/or a crate. Confinement will keep your puppy safe when you cannot watch him.

**Key points:**

- Prevention exercises and management are necessary to successfully integrate your puppy into your household.
- The prevention of behavior problems is easier than treatment.
- Many behaviors we find problematic are normal behaviors of dogs.
- Puppy proof your house.

## Schedule and Routine

Maintaining a schedule and routine for interaction with puppies and adult dogs improves behavioral wellness.

**Key points:**

- Feed your dog at specific times rather than providing access to food all day.
- Walk your dog on leash at least twice a day.
- Train your dog twice a day using positive reinforcement.
- Provide a variety of toys and rotate them to maintain novelty.

- Feed your dog regular scheduled meals in his confinement area. Ideally, all dogs should be meal-fed twice a day rather than fed free choice. Feeding him in his confinement area allows for a positive association with the location. Offer meals at set times and remove the bowl after 20 minutes. If your dog does not finish his meal, pick the food up when he is not underfoot and offer it again at the next meal time. Your dog will learn the routine. Very young or small puppies (less than 5 pounds) may require more frequent meals, up to 3 to 4 times a day. Consult with your veterinarian regarding diets that are suitable for growing puppies. Overfeeding can lead to obesity and future skeletal and health problems. Unfortunately, an estimated 44% of dogs are obese and a few extra pounds on a dog equates to a person being 30 to 50 pounds overweight.[1] Meal feeding twice a day is always preferable to free-choice feeding.

- Walk your dog on leash off your property at least twice a day. Short walks (10 to 20 minutes) off your property allow for socialization and prevent fear and anxiety. Your dog is less likely to develop cabin fever if allowed to see and smell things other than your own backyard.

- Train your dog twice a day using positive reinforcement (treats). Short training sessions (5 to 10 minutes) allow for mental stimulation. The more cues your dog knows and the more eager he is to perform them, the easier he is to manage in any situation.

- Rotate toys in the environment regularly so they maintain novelty. If your dog is preoccupied interacting with appropriate toys, he is less likely to be performing undesirable behaviors. Chew toys are especially important when your puppy is teething.

# Rules of the Household

Puppy parents should define the rules of the household and set realistic expectations for their dog. What is acceptable in your house is a personal decision. A family meeting to discuss and decide on the rules of the house, as well as providing written "Rules of the House for the Dog" will help all family members be successful. Setting rules of the household from early puppyhood and following them allows for consistency and predictability. If the rules are constantly changing, your dog will be unable to understand which behaviors are acceptable. Set rules as guidelines to be followed and try to anticipate future changes in your lifestyle.

**Key points:**

• Determine realistic expectations for your dog and set the rules of your house.

• Rules of the house help provide consistency and predictability.

When setting rules, ask yourself these questions:

• Will the puppy be allowed on furniture?

• Will the puppy sleep in your bed?

• Will the puppy have full access or limited access in the house?

• Will food scraps be given from the table or in the kitchen?

# Problem Solving Model

There will be behaviors your dog performs that you will find undesirable, even though these behaviors may be normal and quite desirable from your dog's perspective. Always view problem behaviors first from the dog's perspective and second from the human perspective. Determining the motivation and the consequence of the behavior will aid in prevention, management, and/or elimination of the behavior. A step-by-step approach can help you problem solve these behaviors.

## Step 1: Identify the ABCs

**Antecedent:** Trigger(s) for the behavior.

**Behavior:** Actual problem or undesirable behavior the dog performs.

**Consequence:** Dog's perceived consequence of the behavior.

**A.** What is the trigger or stimuli that induce the behavior(s)? The antecedent may be related to a social interaction (human or another animal), a sound, or an inanimate object. Multiple triggers may be identified and the antecedent may be context specific. Ask yourself, what is the specific situation in which the behavior occurs? At times, the antecedent is not identifiable and may be related to the dog's internal motivation or needs. For example, your puppy may be hungry and the temptation of a sandwich just within his reach may be irresistible.

**B.** Defining the behavior is crucial to solving the problem. What is the problem or undesirable behavior? Looking at your dog's body language and having an understanding of normal and abnormal behavior is helpful. The actual behavior may give insight to the antecedent or trigger, especially when it is related to internal motivation.

**C.** The consequence of the behavior should be viewed from the dog's perspective. Initially, ask yourself, what did your dog get out of the situation? Secondarily, especially in social contexts, ask how the consequence of the behavior affects others?

## Step 2: Motivation

Identifying the ABCs will often give insight into the motivation. Dogs are amoral, opportunistic, and self centered. They are not spiteful or malicious. In order to simplify motivation, the behavior will be either self rewarding for the dog or human reinforced. Is the behavior self rewarding to the dog? Self-rewarding behaviors offer an immediate benefit to your puppy or dog. For example, a full bladder is emptied and the puppy feels better. Am I rewarding the behavior in some way? Human reinforced behaviors generally relate to behaviors that are socially motivated and reinforced by human attention. For example, a mouthing and jumping puppy is looked at, talked to, and petted.

## Step 3: Prevention or Management

Once the ABCs and motivation have been determined, the ability to prevent or manage the behavior should be explored. Can you *prevent or manage* the behavior in a humane way? For example, can you supervise your puppy or confine him so the majority of eliminations are only on a preferred substrate (outside)? Can you avoid access to the pantry or shoe closet? Prevention and management controls the learning environment and sets your puppy up to succeed. However, it does not address the underlying motivation or change the behavior.

## Step 4: Problem Solving

If the behavior cannot be prevented or managed, then there are two options. These options depend on whether the dog's motivation is self rewarding or reinforced by humans.

### Ignoring

If the motivation and consequence of the behavior is human attention, the behavior should be ignored. If the reward for the behavior is social interaction, i.e., he jumps on you and you push him away, he nudges you and you pet him, he barks and you let him out of his crate, it is likely that ignoring your dog in these situations will cause the learned behavior to cease. Ignoring means not looking at, talking to, or touching your dog at these times. Initially, the attention-getting behavior will worsen because in the past it has always worked, but if you continue to ignore the behavior, it will extinguish.

### Response Substitution

Behaviors that are self reinforcing or self rewarding cannot be ignored. For example, for the teething puppy, chewing on a chair may provide relief. Since chewing is self rewarding, it cannot be ignored. To apply response substitution follow the next three steps:

1. **Interrupt the behavior by getting your dog's attention.** Call his name in an upbeat tone or clap your hands. The interrupter should not be frightening or an indicator of impending punishment. Don't say "no" because it has a negative connotation and may cause an aversive emotional response.

2. **Cue an alternate appropriate behavio**r that is incompatible with the undesirable one before the problem behavior begins or after interruption of the behavior. Redirect and teach your dog an appropriate behavioral response. For example, the dog that greets people by jumping on them is cued to "sit." The dog cannot jump and sit at the same time.

3. **Reward your dog for the appropriate behavior with a food treat.** You may reward and keep your dog busy with a food-stuffed toy.

Teaching your dog appropriate behaviors or cues such as "come," "sit," and "place" allows for response substitution.

Following the problem solving model will allow you to modify many normal problem behaviors.

**Helpful Hints:**

- Many problem-solving techniques will involve teaching your puppy some basic foundation behaviors.

- We encourage you to begin reading Chapter 7: Introduction to Training and Chapter 8: Foundation Training Exercises.

# PLAY BITING AND MOUTHING

## ABCs and Motivation

Play biting is a normal, natural, and necessary behavior of puppies. Puppies learn to control the pressure of their bite from playing with other puppies. When one puppy bites too hard, the other puppy yelps and stops playing. This ends the play, teaching your puppy bite inhibition. Your puppy needs to learn that mouthing or biting people is not the way to prompt people to play. Dogs will bite for reasons other than play; yet *play* biting is the most common reason in puppies. The motivation for the behavior is play, exploratory, or attention seeking. The consequence is generally some form of attention.

## Prevention and Management

Avoid encouraging your puppy to mouth your hands, clothes, or shoes. Instead provide your puppy with a variety of toys for mouthing. Play with your puppy with a tug toy. Proactively provide and rotate toys in the environment for entertainment. Manage or confine your puppy when you are unable to address play biting.

## Problem Solving

Immediate withdrawal of attention is the most effective method (negative punishment).

1. Avoid "yelping" or verbally acknowledging your puppy's social interaction. Vocalizing may increase your puppy's excitement, inadvertently reinforce the unwanted behavior, or can induce a fear of social interaction.

2. The instant your puppy touches your skin or clothes with his teeth, freeze and slowly withdraw yourself from the situation. Calmly and quietly stand up, fold your arms, look away, and walk away. This should be your immediate and consistent response.

When the behavior results in torn clothing or physical injury, you cannot ignore the behavior. Use redirection and reward an alternate appropriate response (response substitution).

3. Calmly and quietly withdraw attention for 2 to 3 seconds.

4. Redirect your puppy to sit or perform any alternate behavior other than mouthing.

5. Reward the sit or behavior by offering a treat or toy.

Do not use any positive punishment through verbal or physical reprimands. Shouting "No," swatting on the nose, grabbing the dog's muzzle, or pinching his lips are counterproductive and often leads to hand- or head-shy dogs. Punishment of play biting does not teach your puppy how to interact appropriately and may cause or contribute to the development of serious aggression.

Consider a typical human social interaction involving talking with one another. If you started to have a conversation with a person and they yelled at you or held your mouth shut, you might stop talking. However, you have now learned to distrust that person because he behaved unpredictably. You have not learned how that person would like you to interact.

1. Mouthing and biting of the hands rather than Sport's blue rubber toy.

2. Immediately ignore the behavior for 2 to 3 seconds by standing up, turning away, and looking away. Then, cue a "sit."

3. Turn and reward the sit with praise and treats.

4. Redirect and reward tugging on appropriate toys.

**Helpful Hints:**

- Mouthing and biting is a normal behavior of growing and adolescent puppies.

- Bite inhibition is learned from interaction with littermates.

- Puppy socialization classes or routine puppy play dates allow puppies to learn to control their bite.

- Anticipate when the behavior is likely to occur and provide appropriate outlets and management.

- Yelling might increase arousal or induce a fear response.

- Withdrawal of attention should be the immediate and consistent response.

- Using a leash and flat buckle collar eases response substitution. Mouthing and biting can be redirected by asking your puppy to "sit" and gently prompting with the leash if necessary.

- If your puppy is constantly demanding attention through mouthing and biting or is over exuberant in his play, he may need increased mental stimulation through positive reinforcement training.

- Reward calm behavior with a small food treat or soft petting. Behaviors that are reinforced will increase in frequency.

- Young children will need adult supervision and help implementing these techniques.

- Biting out of fear is not play biting and should be evaluated by a qualified animal behavior professional immediately.

# TUG OF WAR

## *Importance*

Tug can be an interactive, energetic, and appropriate game to play with your puppy. Playing with your puppy fosters your social relationship. Teaching your puppy to enjoy playing tug with you allows the tug to become a useful tool for motivation and reward. When taught correctly, it allows you to contain and control your dog's arousal. Tug of war is a suitable outlet for play mouthing and biting and teaches your puppy how to play appropriately with people.

### *How to Play Tug of War*

1. You should initiate and end the tug of war game. Any sloppy attempts by your dog to get the toy that make contact with your skin should immediately end the game. You walk away with the toy.

2. Give the verbal cue "take it" and present the tug toy. Move the tug toy slightly back and forth to foster interest or chase.

3. When your dog has the toy in his mouth, engage him in a gentle game of tug. Verbally reward his interest in the tug.

4. Freeze (stop tugging and any toy movement). Give the verbal cue "drop it" and prompt it with a treat directly under your dog's nose. Reward with the treat for dropping the toy. Pick up the toy.

5. Add the cue "sit" or "down," and reward the behavior with "take it" and presentation of the tug toy. This helps to control your puppy's arousal.

6. Repeat the above steps. Eventually, you will delay your presentation of the treat after giving the "drop it" cue.

7. When the game is over, the tug toy should be placed away from your dog.

Teaching your dog to play tug of war will not make him aggressive. Tug can be a physical and mental outlet for energetic dogs. However, do not play tug of war with dogs that guard objects and/or display aggression. We do not recommend children playing tug of war with dogs, because the excitement level may be more difficult to control. This should be an adult-only game.

**Helpful Hints:**

- Your dog may be on leash for control when teaching tug of war.

- A rope or line attached to the tug is sometimes helpful.

See **Chapter 8: Foundation Training Exercises** for teaching the cues:

- "Sit"

- "Down"

- "Bring"

- "Drop it"

1. Offer an appropriate tug toy and tell your puppy to "take it."

2. Motion elicits a chase response.

3. Gentle tension on the tug toy will keep your puppy engaged. Freeze prior to prompting your puppy to release the toy.

4. Offer a treat for relinquishment and then give the cue "take it."

5. Present the toy and play.

6. Calm down the play prior to prompting "drop it."

# JUMPING

## ABCs and Motivation

Jumping is a normal and affectionate greeting behavior of dogs. Puppies learn to solicit attention and feeding through jumping and licking the commissure of their mother's lips and muzzle. This behavior stimulates regurgitation. Puppies jump on people in an attempt to show affection and nuzzle or lick their face. Your puppy needs to learn that jumping on people is not the way to solicit attention. The motivation for the behavior is excitement and social interaction. The consequence is generally some form of attention. Because dogs are social, typical human responses that perpetuate jumping may include an eye glance, a verbal reprimand, physical contact such as pushing the dog off, or any combination of the above.

## Prevention and Management

Avoid encouraging your puppy to jump on you when excited. With over exuberant puppies, social interactions and greetings should be calm. Manage or prevent jumping though the use of a leash in situations when the behavior is likely to occur. Proactively ask your puppy to sit prior to giving attention. Tell him what you want him to do before he makes the undesirable choice of jumping. Teach your puppy that sitting is the behavior that results in people turning, looking at, talking to, and petting him. Thus, the act of sitting becomes an appropriate attention getting behavior. Set your puppy up to be successful. When visitors enter the home, confine your puppy if you are unable to work on teaching an appropriate response. This prevents your puppy from being rewarded for jumping on guests.

## Problem Solving

1. Immediate withdrawal of attention is the most effective method (negative punishment).

2. Avoid verbally or physically acknowledging your puppy's solicitation of attention.

3. The instant your puppy jumps toward you, withdraw any form of attention or reward. This means stepping away, turning away, folding your arms, and looking away. Do not talk to your puppy. If you are sitting, calmly and quietly stand up, fold your arms, and look away. This should be your immediate and consistent response.

When the behavior cannot be ignored, use response substitution. Redirect and reward an alternate appropriate response.

4. Calmly and quietly withdraw attention for 2 to 3 seconds.

5. Redirect your puppy to "sit," "down," or any behavior incompatible with jumping.

6. Reward the alternate behavior with a treat and calm attention. Over exuberant praise is likely to result in your puppy jumping.

Do not use any positive punishment through verbal or physical reprimands. Shouting "No," swatting, pushing, or kneeing are counterproductive and often lead to fearful and shy dogs. Punishment of jumping does not teach your puppy how to interact appropriately and may cause or directly contribute to the development of serious aggression. For example, typical human social interactions involving greeting include shaking a person's hand. If you reached to shake a person's hand and that person yelled at you or pushed you away, you may not want to approach that person in the future and you have learned to distrust that person.

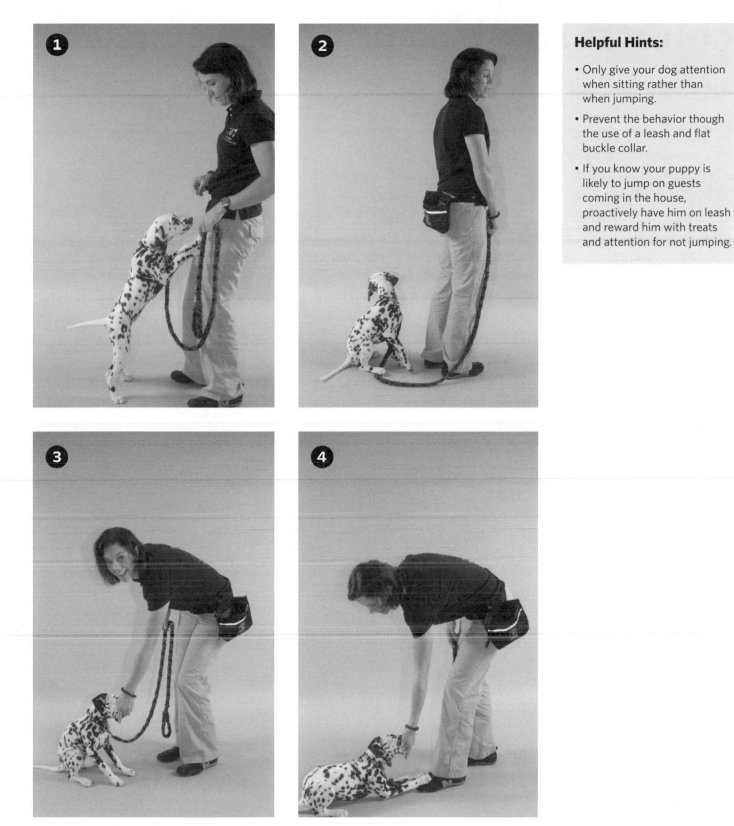

**1.** Puppy jumping up on handler.

**2.** Immediately ignore the behavior for 2 to 3 seconds by turning and looking away.

**3 & 4.** Redirect the puppy to sit or down and reward the alternate response with treats and attention, such as eye contact, calm praise, and petting.

# COUNTER SURFING AND STEALING OBJECTS

### ABCs and Motivation

Dogs are opportunistic and they have a great sense of smell. Dogs are also curious and explore their world with their mouths. You can see how a piece of pizza left on the counter might go missing. Your dog is likely to check out the kitchen counter, trash cans, or coffee table at some point. What he learns when this happens will set the course for future behavior. Motivation can be exploratory or appetitive. It can also develop into an attention-getting behavior. If your dog is stealing objects deliberately in front of you, he may have learned that it gets a reaction from you. On the other hand, many dogs will check the counters, trash can, and tables because they smell food. If this behavior pays off on occasion, this will make for a very strong behavior resistant to extinction. Just like playing the slot machine, sometimes you hit the jackpot. Typical consequences that perpetuate counter surfing and object stealing may include finding food, a game of chase, a verbal reprimand (this is attention), physical contact, or any combination of the above.

### Prevention and Management

Avoid access to the problem area through the use of baby gates or an exercise pen when you cannot supervise. If necessary, supervise or prevent the behavior though the use of a leash or tether (leash restraint holding the dog in place). Do not offer your dog food in the kitchen or from the table. Keep the counters clean and place the trash can in a cupboard or closet. Many covered trash cans are commercially available to help your dog to be successful. Proactively cue your dog to go to his place located outside of the kitchen or away from the table (See Chapter 8 to teach "Place"). Teach your dog that resting on his bed is the place to be when you are in the kitchen or sitting at the table. Give your dog a frozen food storage device (toy) while he is on his bed to keep him busy. Confine your dog when you are unable to teach an appropriate response.

### Problem Solving

*If your dog is checking out the counter and there is nothing he can get.* Ignore the behavior. This is a normal exploratory behavior and if you respond to it, you are likely to reinforce the behavior with attention. Behaviors that are reinforced will increase in frequency. If the counter checking does not pay off, the behavior will cease.

*If there are items within his reach.* Use response substitution. Clap your hands to get your dog's attention, give him

1. Prevention with the use of a baby gate to block access to the kitchen.

2. Dog taught to rest on a bed ("place") when people are in the kitchen.

3. Dog stealing towel off counter in front of owner.

4. Dog relinquishes object on cue and earns a reward.

a cue you have previously taught ("leave it," "place," "sit," "come"), and reward him for the alternate behavior.

*If your dog has a stolen object?* Avoid chasing him because this just makes for a fun game of "keep away" and increases your dog's perceived value of the object.

- *A low-value object* (paper towel, tissue) that is unlikely to cause harm—ignore him. Do not look at him or say anything. Leave the room. He may follow you. Remind yourself to be more careful to manage those situations in the future.

- *A high-value object* (cell phone, wallet, candy bar) that may cause harm—you have three options:

1. Response substitution: If you have already taught your dog to bring and drop objects on cue, prompt these behaviors and reward.

2. Distraction: If you have not already taught the "bring" and "drop it" cues, then distract your dog by being animated and running away from him. You might grab his favorite toy or a treat and act like you are having fun without him. Because dogs are social, this may prompt your dog to check out what you are doing and leave the stolen object.

3. Exchange: If your dog is not distracted by your attempts to be more exciting, then prompt him to release the object with a special treat such as a piece of cheese, hotdog, or sandwich meat. Lead your dog away from the object by giving him several treats. Once you have him in another room or outside, return to pick up the object without him underfoot. The exchange should not substitute for teaching your dog to willingly relinquish objects.

Verbal or physical reprimands will only teach your dog to steal objects when you are not around, to run away from you, and will increase the dog's perceived value of the object.

Commercial pet deterrents are available, but they should not be used as a first-option strategy. Gadgets and gizmos are never a substitute for teaching an appropriate response and they can have unpleasant side effects, eliciting fear and anxiety in your dog.

**Helpful Hints:**

- Initially, use a tether to keep your dog on his bed when unsupervised to keep him away from the kitchen/table.

- Proactively offer your dog a food-stuffed toy prior to cooking or eating dinner.

- Teach your dog to eagerly bring and release objects from his mouth.

# CHEWING

## ABCs and Motivation

Destructive chewing is a common behavior problem of puppies. The motivation is often a normal exploratory behavior of puppies and adolescent dogs. Chewing may be associated with teething or recreational exploration of the world with their mouths. If the chewing is excessive or only associated with your departure, contact your veterinarian.

## Prevention and Management

Management and supervision are extremely important to prevent your dog from developing undesirable chewing habits. Use a puppy-proofed confinement area at times when you are unable to supervise. Block access to your puppy's favorite inappropriate chew items.

- Lack of stimulation may lead to excessive chewing. Provide your puppy with routine walks, play time, and training.

- Reward and encourage chewing on appropriate objects. Understand your dog's perspective. To him, everything is a potential chew toy.

- Avoid offering objects to chew that are concentrated with human scent because it teaches your puppy to chew objects that smell like you. He will not know the difference between an old or new pair of shoes.

- Provide a variety of appropriate chew toys and rotate them. Rotating toys maintains novelty and increases the likelihood your puppy will play with them.

There are numerous commercially available chew toys. Despite manufacturer claims, no toy is indestructible. Dogs can destroy and ingest a toy very quickly. Hard rubber toys are more resistant to destruction. When offering your puppy a new toy, monitor him closely. Check your dog's toys daily for damage. Toys will become damaged or worn over time and will need to be replaced periodically.

## Problem Solving

Chewing cannot be ignored because the behavior is self rewarding. Use response substitution:

1. Call your dog's name in an upbeat tone or clap your hands to get his attention.

2. Call him to you.

3. Provide an appropriate chew toy.

Be proactive. If you see your puppy getting ready to chew on a chair leg, redirect him to an appropriate hard chew toy before he makes the undesirable choice.

Verbal or physical reprimands will only teach your dog that it is unsafe to chew the chair when you are around. He will instead do it in your absence. Make chewing on appropriate objects more rewarding. It may be necessary to make inappropriate objects aversive through the use of a commercially available taste deterrent. Develop good chewing habits through management, supervision, and providing appropriate chewing alternatives.

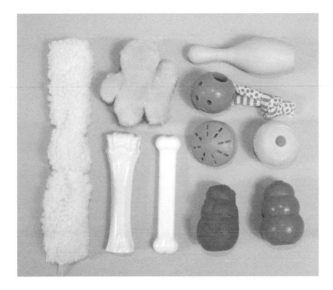

Examples of appropriate chew toys:

Hard rubber or plastic chew toys

Balls (appropriate size)

Food storage toys

Fleece soft toys (with supervision)

**Helpful Hints:**

- If your puppy is chewing a hard object and you redirect him to a soft chew toy, this is not as likely to appease his motivation. Instead, offer a hard chew toy.

- Avoid giving your dog meat bones, pig ears, and hooves. These items may be dangerous if ingested. Avoid offering human articles such as old socks or shoes. Your dog will not know the difference between new and old ones.

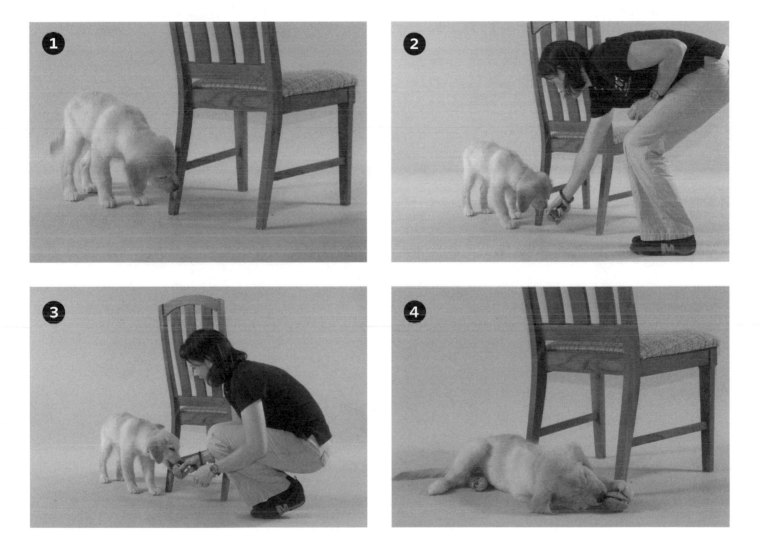

**1.** Puppy chewing on a chair leg.

**2.** Interrupt the behavior by calling your puppy's name in an upbeat tone.

**3.** Offer an appropriate chew toy/food storage device.

**4.** Successful redirection.

# DIGGING

## ABCs and Motivation

Digging can occur for a multitude of reasons. The motivation can include:

1. *Thermoregulation:* To keep warm or cool when outside for prolonged periods of time.

2. *Hunting:* Insects or other animals. Dogs can smell and hear animals in the ground.

3. *Burying:* Hiding a treasured item to be recovered later.

4. *Escape or anxiety:* This usually involves digging along a fence line. For example, a dog may become panicked by a thunderstorm or an intact male dog may be motivated to roam the neighborhood.

Some breeds of dogs are more likely to dig than others. Terriers are notorious for being diggers. Terrier comes from the Latin word "terra," meaning "of the earth." Many terrier and some hound breeds have been selectively bred to dig and chase vermin under ground. Regardless of your dog's breeding, all dogs have the potential to dig.

It is a self-rewarding behavior. Provide an appropriate place to dig. Make inappropriate digging spots aversive by placing your dog's feces in the hole. Redirect your dog to an alternate appropriate behavior.

## Prevention and Management

Manage your dog by not allowing unsupervised access to favorite digging areas. Lack of stimulation may lead to excessive digging. Provide scheduled walks, play time, and training. Time in the backyard alone should not be a substitute for human initiated exercise and interactions.

Provide your dog with an appropriate place to dig. Similar to a sand box for a child, a digging box for your dog can provide him with hours of appropriate digging entertainment. Make the digging location enticing to your dog by hiding treats in the substrate and rewarding him for showing interest in the digging spot.

## Problem Solving

Digging cannot be ignored because the behavior is self rewarding. Use response substitution:

1. In an upbeat tone, call your dog's name or clap your hands to get his attention.

2. Call him to you.

3. Redirect him to an appropriate digging area, a short game of play, or other incompatible behavior and reward.

Be proactive. If you see your puppy getting ready to dig, redirect him before he makes the undesirable choice.

Verbal or physical reprimands will only teach your dog that it is unsafe to dig in front of you. He will do it in your absence instead. Do not leave him unsupervised in the yard.

Placing your dog's feces in the unwanted digging spot will make that area unattractive. However, without supervision, management, and appropriate alternatives, your dog will find a new location to dig.

Digging is a normal behavior of dogs that is found to be undesirable to people.

A children's sand box can provide an appropriate outlet for the digging dog.

**Helpful Hints:**

- Placing your dog's feces in undesired digging locations will make those areas unattractive for most dogs.

- If digging is excessive, only associated with your departure, or the result of a panicked dog, a behavior consultation with a qualified animal behavior professional is warranted.

**1.** Let your dog observe you burying his favorite toy or treat in the digging box.

**2.** Foster interest in the digging box with verbal encouragement, "dig, dig, dig."

**3.** Finding buried treasure, a food-stuffed toy.

**4.** Appropriate digging is reinforced with the opportunity to dig and finding treasures.

# CONFINEMENT TRAINING

Confinement training refers to teaching your puppy that he has a safe and secure area of his own in which to relax. Confinement keeps your puppy safe when you cannot directly supervise him.

A crate is a valuable tool for house training and management. When traveling with your dog by car or air, a crate provides safety and is often necessary. Teaching your dog to be comfortable and relaxed in a crate should be done as soon as possible. Your puppy's crate is a place for him to get away from the crazy human world.

An exercise pen can prevent destructive behavior while giving your puppy a bit more freedom. This is similar to a play pen for toddlers. The crate may be placed within or attached to the exercise pen. Toys and water should be made available in this area. The exercise pen may be used for short periods of time while you are home. An exercise pen with an elimination area may be utilized if you are forced to leave your puppy for an extended period of time (see Chapter 6: House Training).

## Types of Crates

Wire and plastic are the two most common crate types. Fold-up wire crates are easy to transport and allow superior ventilation, but some puppies prefer the closed in den-like area of plastic crates. When considering the purchase of a crate, if you plan to travel with your dog, it will be beneficial to determine if the crate is airline approved.

The crate should be large enough for your puppy to get up, stretch, turn around, and lie down. If your puppy will be a large dog, it is a good idea to purchase a crate that will accommodate his adult size. However, your puppy may eliminate in a crate that is too large. Therefore, a crate divider should be used to prevent elimination. Once your dog is house trained, a larger crate is preferred to provide more freedom.

## When to Use the Confinement Area

Your puppy should be in the crate or exercise pen whenever you cannot directly supervise him. Occasionally, life will become very hectic. You may be trying to take care of the children, fixing breakfast, getting school supplies together, or talking on the phone. Meanwhile, your puppy is grabbing food off the table, stealing and chewing a pair of socks, and basically learning inappropriate behavior. The confinement area should be used to manage your puppy so that he doesn't have opportunities to learn inappropriate behaviors. Control what your puppy is learning.

Provide mental and physical exercise when the puppy is out of his confinement area. This may be accomplished through scheduled training, play, and walks. Alternatively, to teach your puppy to be calm in other parts of the house, have him on leash and with you whenever possible. While watching television, have your puppy next to you on leash and give him a special toy or food storage device to keep him occupied. Using a tether teaches him in a controlled manner how to acclimate to the human domestic environment.

The crate should be used throughout your dog's life. The amount of time your dog will spend in the crate will decrease as he develops. The crate is a great place to feed your dog his meals. Plan to use the crate regularly for at least the first few years.

## *Teach Your Puppy to Love Confinement*

- Confinement areas should be located in commonly used areas of the home. If your puppy's confinement area is in a spare bedroom or unused area of the house, he is less likely to enjoy spending time in it.

- Always give your puppy a treat for going to his confinement area.

- A food-stuffed storage device will entertain your puppy for a longer period of time. Offer it to your puppy when he is in his crate. This is comparable to giving your children a video game to play in their bedroom.

- Hide treats daily in the confinement area. When your puppy explores the area he will begin to believe in the crate fairy.

- Going into the confinement area should always be fun. Use an upbeat tone and attitude rather than a threatening or scolding manner when confining your puppy.

- Never punish your dog by sending him to his crate.

- Supply your puppy with appropriate toys in his confinement area.

- Feed your puppy his meals in the crate with the door opened or closed.

- If your puppy is vocalizing in his confinement area, wait for him to quiet down before you let him out or give him any attention (verbal, physical, or eye contact).

- Place your puppy in the crate at times even when you are home. This will teach your puppy that the crate does not always signal that you are leaving the house.

- Minimize the length of time your puppy is in his confinement area by offering scheduled breaks. Generally, an acceptable time line is your puppy's age in months + 1 hour (example: 2 months of age + 1 hour = 3 hours maximum). Excessive confinement will result in hyperactivity.

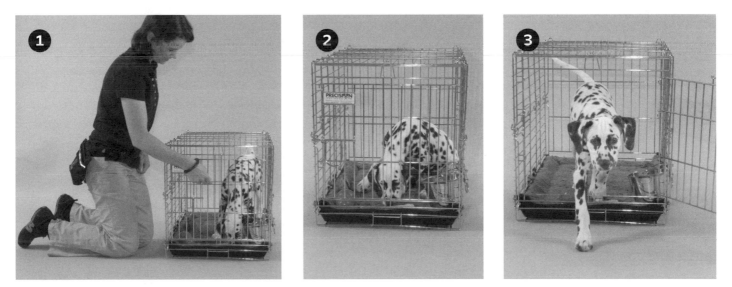

1. Offer a food storage device or treat every time your puppy is confined.
2. Hiding treats, toys, and providing soft bedding makes confinement a positive experience.
3. Let your puppy explore the crate with the door open in order to find goodies, and only let him out if quiet.

# INDEPENDENCE TRAINING

Dogs are social animals; it is not natural for them to be left alone for extended periods of time. Most puppies will show some mild signs of stress when first separated from their mother and littermates. Separation anxiety is a common disorder of dogs manifesting in codependence. Dogs with separation anxiety show signs of distress and may panic when separated from their attachment figure. Often the attachment figure is a person, but occasionally it can be another pet. These distress signs may include barking, whining, howling, pacing, drooling, destructive chewing, and urinating or defecating when left alone or confined away from people. The motivation for the behavior is panic and an intense desire for social interaction. The consequence is generally some form of attention since dogs are social. Typical human responses that perpetuate codependence may include talking to or letting your dog out of his confinement area when barking, always giving your dog attention when he solicits it, practicing elaborate greetings and departures, a lack of independence training, or any combination of the above.

Separation anxiety is the most common behavioral disorder of dogs. It may develop at any age. The condition can sometimes be prevented by appropriate interactions early in puppy development. However, there can be a genetic or learned component.

## Teach Your Puppy Independence

- Although it is important to socialize your puppy, puppies need time home alone.
- Teaching a young dog to be comfortable when home alone will initially involve confinement for safety.
- Give your dog a frozen, food-stuffed toy every time he is confined or left alone.
- Hide treats and toys in his confinement area for positive associations.
- Dogs should be confined at times when people are home to prevent an association of being locked away only when people leave the home.
- Arrivals and departures to and from the home should be calm and nonchalant. Avoid high arousal and elaborate hellos and goodbyes.
- Teaching your dog a relaxed sit or down/stay is an exercise of independence.

Separation anxiety can escalate quickly and the condition is unlikely to go away without treatment. Signs may occur when you are away from home or your dog is confined behind a barrier. If you are concerned that your dog may be exhibiting separation anxiety, contact your veterinarian immediately for a behavioral appointment.

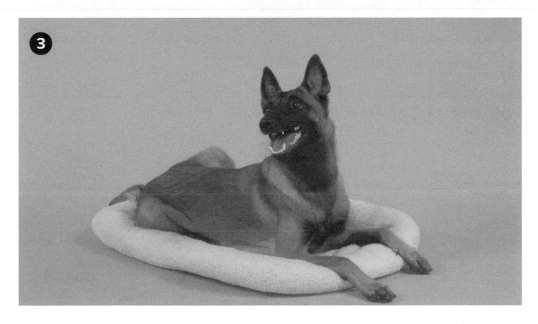

1. Separation anxiety may include chewing objects in your absence.

2. Teaching your dog to be comfortable in your absence will involve teaching him to be comfortable when confined in your presence.

3. Teaching a down-stay is an independence exercise.

# FOOD BOWL EXERCISES

To prevent food bowl aggression, feed your puppy in a low-traffic area and pick up the bowl when he is out of sight. If your puppy or adult dog has never shown aggression over his food, teach him to enjoy having people around his food by feeding him by hand or by tossing special treats into the bowl when he is eating. Most dogs do not like to be petted while eating.

It is somewhat normal for a dog to defend its food from other animals in the home. In multi-pet households, it is best to provide each pet with his own feeding location. Dogs should be fed from separate bowls in separate locations of the home. This minimizes social competition over food as a resource. Feeding meals in the crate at set times allows for safe management and a positive association with the crate.

Aggression over food towards people in puppies is a red flag predicting human-directed aggression later in life. Your puppy is not going through a phase and is unlikely to grow out of the behavior. Consult with your veterinarian or seek a referral to a qualified animal behavior professional immediately if your dog is showing aggression towards people over food.

## Teach Your Puppy to be Comfortable with People near the Food Bowl

1. Other pets in the household should be out of sight or confined prior to implementing the exercise.

2. Place a few kibbles in the bowl and place the bowl on the ground. Allow the puppy to eat all the food. Pick up the empty bowl and place a few more kibbles in the bowl. Repeat until the entire meal is fed.

3. Another variation: Start with a few kibbles in the bowl and as the puppy is eating add a few more kibbles to the bowl until the entire meal is fed.

4. Toss a special treat in the bowl from a distance as you enter the room in which your dog is eating. This teaches your dog that human presence means something better will fall from the sky. It is a positive association with your presence.

When doing food bowl exercises, we want your puppy to learn that people around the bowl are not a threat. Never pull the food bowl away from your dog while he is eating. Repeatedly removing the food bowl or food while your dog is eating does not teach him to be comfortable with people near his bowl. To the contrary, your dog will anticipate your presence means the food is going away. This is a negative association with your presence. People should strive to be the giver of food and never the taker.

**If your puppy has shown aggression towards you over the food bowl, do not attempt these exercises. Contact a qualified animal behavior professional immediately.**

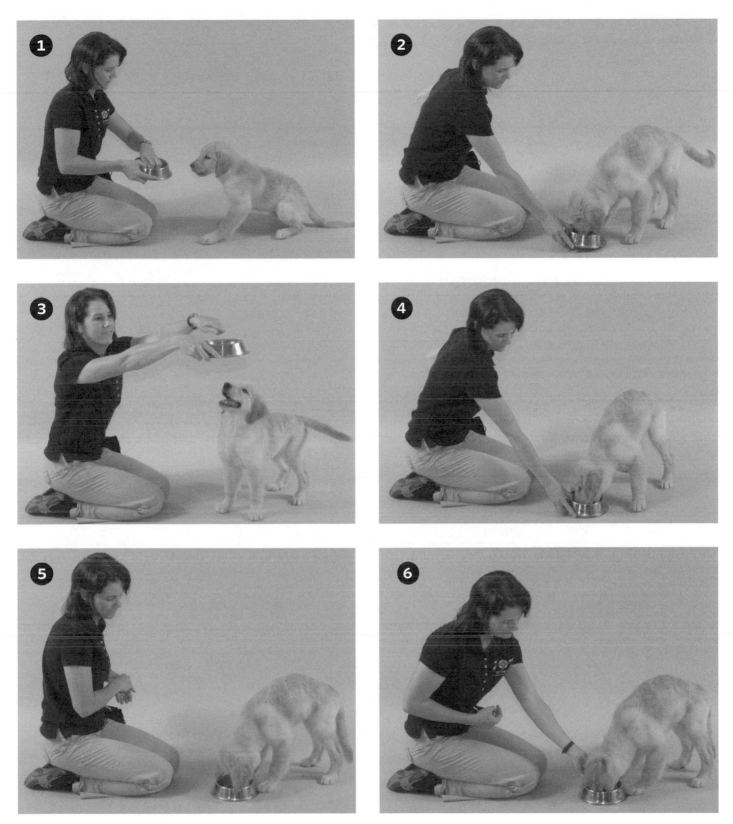

1. Place a few kibbles in the bowl.

2. Place the bowl on the ground. Allow the puppy to eat all the food.

3. Pick up the empty bowl and place a few more kibbles in the bowl.

4. Lower the bowl to the ground and allow the puppy to eat all the food.

5 & 6. Add special treats or more kibble to the bowl while your puppy is eating.

# HANDLING EXERCISES

Handling refers to manipulating or touching parts of your dog's body, such as his ears, mouth, nose, tail, feet, etc. Handling may be performed with a hand or a brush.

To make handling less aversive, your dog should learn to associate being touched with earning treats. Although many dogs will tolerate being handled, making it a pleasant experience rather than a neutral or an aversive experience is necessary to make future experiences less traumatic to your dog.

Clicker or marker training can be very effective in desensitizing a dog to being handled. We recommend conditioning your dog to the clicker and training some behaviors with clicker training prior to working on these exercises (see Chapter 7: Introduction to Training).

## Teach Your Puppy to be Comfortable with Handling

- Your puppy should be calm and relaxed before starting these exercises.

- Use small easily consumed treats and have your clicker ready.

- Keep sessions short; 1 to 5 minutes.

- Go slow and make it fun and positive (a negative experience could have a long-lasting negative consequence).

- Desensitization and counter conditioning will be utilized to facilitate relaxation with handling.

- Begin by touching your dog gently in a specific spot for 1 second. Click while you are touching him. Remove your hand. Give your dog a treat. Body parts to touch include:

  | | | | |
  |---|---|---|---|
  | • Head | • Neck | • Chest | • Legs |
  | • Ears | • Shoulders | • Belly | • Feet |
  | • Nose | • Back | • Flank | |
  | • Mouth | • Tail | • Elbows | |

- After your dog is relaxed and comfortable with you gently touching him for 1 second on the various body parts, then increase to 2 seconds, 3 seconds, 4 seconds, etc.

- Gradually increase the pressure of the touch and decrease the duration of contact. Reset duration to 1 second. Click while you are touching, then remove your hand, and offer a treat. Gradually increase the level of pressure.

- Use one hand to touch and the other hand for the clicker. Avoid clicking near your dog's ears.

**If your dog has shown aggression or extreme fear with handling, do not attempt these exercises. Contact a qualified animal behavior professional immediately.**

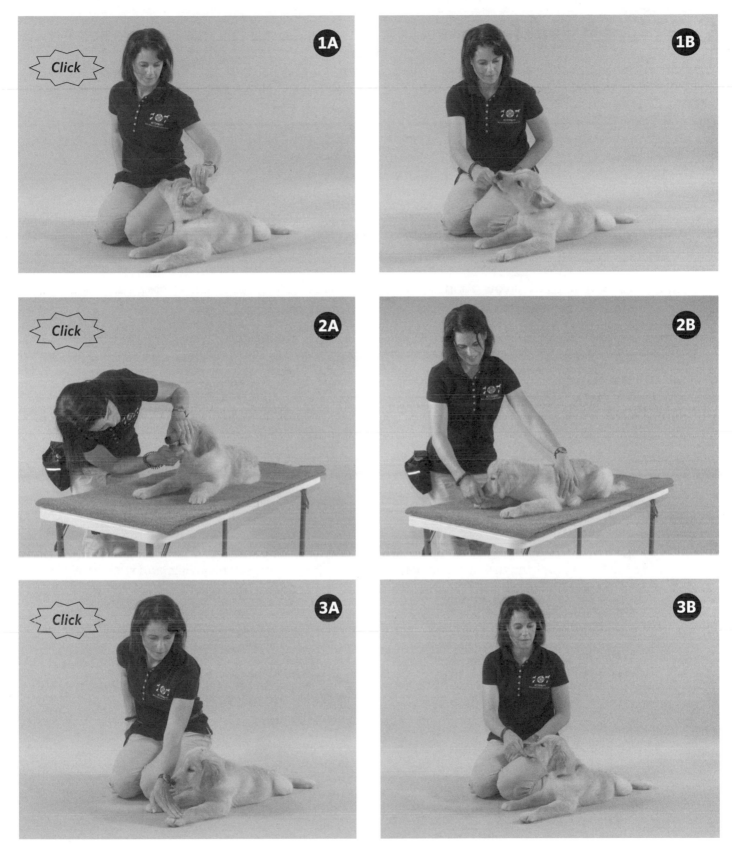

**1A.** Click while touching the ear. **1B.** Release the ear and offer a treat.

**2A.** Click while manipulating the mouth. **2B.** Release the mouth and offer a treat.

**3A.** Click while touching the paw. **3B.** Release the paw and offer a treat.

# GOTCHA GAME

The Gotcha Game prevents your puppy from shying away when your reach for his collar. Nothing is more frustrating than reaching for your puppy only to have him back away just out of your reach. Gotcha teaches your puppy to be comfortable and to like having his collar manipulated.

Clicker or marker training can be very effective in desensitizing a dog to being gently restrained by the collar. Read about clicker training in Chapter 7 prior to working on this exercise.

### Teach Your Puppy to Enjoy Having his Collar Handled

1. Slowly reach out toward your puppy. Click with the extension of your arm. Withdraw your arm and give a food treat.

2. Slowly reach for and touch your puppy's collar. Click while touching the collar. Remove your hand and give a treat. Be careful not to click too close to your puppy's ear. Repeat.

3. When you know your puppy is unlikely to shy away with being reached for or touched, add the verbal cue, "Collar." Say the cue, "Collar," then reach for and touch the collar, click and treat. Using a cue tells your dog what you are about to do. It makes your behavior more predictable.

4. Give the cue "Collar." Slowly reach for and touch your puppy's collar. Gently place one or two fingers under the collar. Click while holding the collar. Release the collar and give a treat. Repeat.

5. Gradually increase the length of time you hold the collar before clicking.

6. Apply slight tension to the collar. Click during the tension. Release the collar and give a treat.

7. Gradually increase the amount of manipulation to the collar. Click during the manipulation. Release the collar and give a treat.

8. Periodically throughout the day, walk up behind your puppy, gently grab his collar, and stick a treat in his mouth at the same time.

Your puppy should love having his collar grabbed because it has been repeatedly associated with food rewards.

Avoid grabbing your dog's collar roughly and excessive manipulation prior to desensitization. If you only grab your dog's collar when you are about to do something that he perceives as aversive, it will have a negative connotation.

**Helpful Hints:**

• Use desensitization. Avoid eliciting a fear response or struggle from your puppy by progressing with gotcha gradually.

• If you progress too rapidly and your puppy struggles slightly, do not let him go. Wait for him to relax, click, and then release him and offer a food treat.

• A light leash or tab may also be used to work on gotcha; this is helpful for the dog who is more reluctant to being reached for.

Periodically throughout the day, walk up to your dog, gently grab his collar, and place a treat in his mouth.

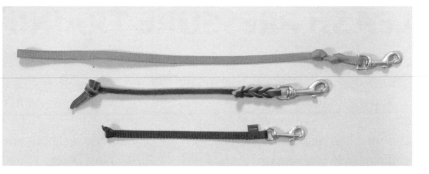

Examples of leash tabs: 8 to 16 inches in length

Sport receiving a treat while having his collar manipulated.

1. Touch the collar and click while handling.

2. Release your hand from the collar and offer a treat.

Click

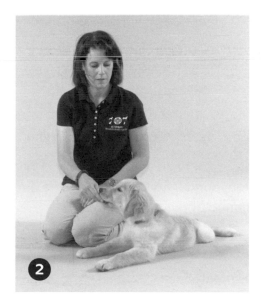

**If your dog has shown aggression with handling his collar, do not attempt these exercises. Contact a qualified animal behavior professional.**

# LEASH PRESSURE TRAINING

Leash pressure training teaches your puppy to be guided and to go with pressure on his collar. Dogs have a natural opposition reflex. This means that when a puppy feels tension by a leash attached to his collar, the natural response is to pull backward against the tension. The goal of leash pressure training is to teach your dog to go in the direction of the tension in anticipation of a food reward. This changes your dog's emotional and physical response when he feels tension on the leash. Leash pressure training prevents your dog from pulling while walking on leash.

To begin training, you will need a light leash or tab connected to your puppy's flat buckle collar. A clicker and treats are necessary to mark and reinforce going in the direction of leash pressure. You should have already been practicing the Gotcha Game and read about clicker training in Chapter 7 prior to working on this exercise.

## Teach Your Puppy to Go with Leash Pressure

1. Apply steady gentle pressure to your dog's leash tab on a horizontal plane. You should prevent your dog from moving in the opposite direction against the leash pressure. While you remain stationary, click the instant your dog takes a step in the direction of the leash pressure. Release the pressure and give a treat.

2. Apply steady gentle pressure to your dog's leash tab on a horizontal plane (forward). At the same time you apply the leash pressure, take a step forward. Click the instant your dog takes a step forward with you. Release the pressure and give a treat.

3. Apply steady gentle pressure to your dog's leash tab in a horizontal plane (backward). At the same time you apply the leash pressure, take a step backward. Click the instant your dog takes a step backward with you. Release the pressure and give a treat.

4. The cue to your dog is gentle tension on the leash which means to move in that direction in anticipation of a food reward.

5. Gradually progress to 1 step, 2 steps, or 3 steps prior to clicking. Tension on the leash should be released after the first step and not sustained. Reward moving in the desired direction with a food treat.

Your puppy should move with the tension on his collar in anticipation of a food reward. This conditions a positive emotional response in your dog when he feels leash pressure.

Do not jerk on your dog's collar when teaching this exercise. The leash pressure is not a correction, but a cue for your dog to take a step in the direction of pressure. We do not want leash pressure to have a negative connotation for your dog.

**Helpful Hints:**

• Practicing forward and backwards is best accomplished with your dog between you and a wall such that your dog can only move forward or backward.

• Tension on the leash/collar should always be delivered on a horizontal plane rather than a vertical plane.

**✗ Incorrect form.**

Notice the leash pressure is in a vertical plane; being pulled up and back.

**✔ Correct form.**

Notice the leash pressure is on a horizontal plane.

**1A.** Horizontal tension on collar tab. **1B.** Click when your dog steps forward. **1C.** Release tension and treat.

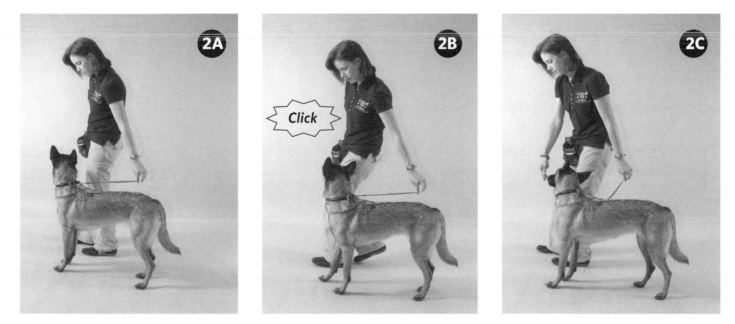

**2A.** Horizontal tension on collar tab. **2B.** Click when your dog steps backward. **2C.** Release tension and treat.

# RESTRAINT TRAINING

Restraint refers to physically holding a dog still and is often used during routine veterinary procedures. Dogs learn very quickly that something unpleasant is about to happen when they are restrained. Through experience, they learn that when held still, they may have their nails trimmed, temperature taken, vaccinations given, blood drawn, ears cleaned, or body groomed. No wonder many dogs try to avoid it! Through desensitization and counter conditioning many handling procedures can be performed with little or no restraint. However, there will be times when your dog will need to hold completely still.

Clicker or marker training can be very effective in desensitizing a dog to being restrained. Read about clicker training in Chapter 7 prior to working on these exercises.

## *Teach Your Puppy to be Comfortable with Restraint*

- Your puppy should be calm and relaxed before starting these exercises. Consider starting on the floor or you may use a table for a small dog.

- Use special, readily consumed treats, such as canned cheese.

- Keep sessions short; 1 to 2 minutes.

- Go slow and make it fun and positive (a negative experience could have long-lasting negative consequences).

- Gently place an arm around your puppy and click. Release and offer a treat. Arm goes over his back and under the belly/chest.

- Progress to cradling with one arm over his back and under his belly/chest and the other arm under his neck.

- With each consecutive repetition, gradually increase the pressure and/or duration.

- If while performing these exercises your puppy struggles to get down, follow these steps:

  1. Continue to hold him.

  2. Say nothing.

  3. Wait until he calms down.

  4. Give him a treat.

  5. Put him down.

  6. Next time progress slower to avoid stress and struggling.

**If your dog has shown aggression or extreme fear with restraint, do not attempt these exercises. Contact a qualified animal behavior professional.**

**Helpful Hints:**

- Use desensitization. Avoid eliciting a fear response or struggle from your puppy by progressing with restraint gradually. Click and release your puppy when he is relaxed.

- If you progress too rapidly and your puppy struggles slightly, do not let him go. Wait for him to relax, click, and then release him and offer a food treat.

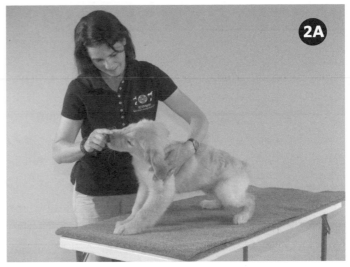

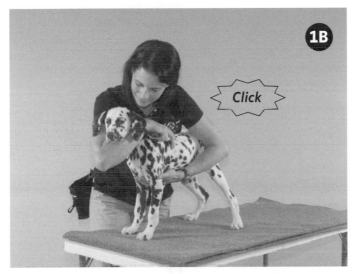

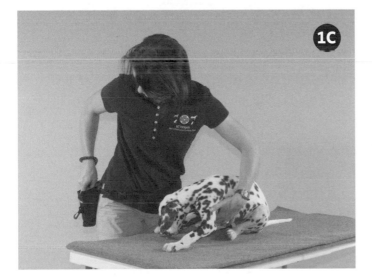

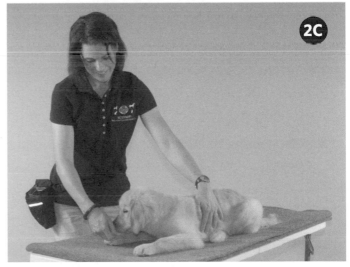

**1A.** Place a hand on your puppy's chest and simultaneously offer a food treat.

**1B.** Gently restrain as shown. Click.

**1C.** Release and reward with a food treat.

**2A.** Place a hand on your puppy's chest and simultaneously offer a food treat.

**2B.** Lift your puppy slightly. Click.

**2C.** Release and reward with a food treat.

# MUZZLE TRAINING

Teaching your puppy to be comfortable and to enjoy wearing a basket muzzle can be a useful skill. You never know if your dog will need to wear one in the future, as accidents can happen and most dogs will bite when in pain. Muzzles are often first introduced to dogs at times of high stress or during veterinary procedures where there is a concern about safety. Dogs quickly learn when they see the muzzle that something unpleasant is about to happen to them. This is not the ideal time for your dog's first experience with a muzzle. Rather, your dog's first experience with a muzzle should be a positive one. Muzzle training prevents and reduces stress when a muzzle is necessary and improves the safety of all involved.

We recommend using a plastic or wire basket muzzle rather than a cloth one. Basket muzzles are safer for your dog because they allow him to pant and regulate his body temperature. Holes in the basket also allow the administration of treats for counter conditioning. Through desensitization and counter conditioning, most dogs learn to love their muzzle.

Clicker or marker training can be very effective in desensitizing a dog to a basket muzzle. Read about clicker training in Chapter 7 prior to working on these exercises.

## *Teach Your Puppy to be Comfortable Wearing a Basket Muzzle*

1. Introduce the basket muzzle with food treats. Let your dog see you place peanut butter or canned cheese into the nose of the muzzle.

2. Present the muzzle and allow your dog to approach and place his nose in the muzzle. Your dog should approach at his own pace. Keep your hand still and avoid moving the muzzle towards your dog. Reaching forward is likely to make your dog back away.

3. Once your dog is eagerly eating treats out of the muzzle, begin to slowly back away from him with the muzzle. This forces him to move forward in order to keep his nose in the muzzle and continue consuming rewards.

4. Remove the muzzle (slowly lift it up and away) prior to consumption of all the treats and subsequent backing out of the muzzle. Once the muzzle is attached, he will not be able to back out of the muzzle. You do not want him to practice backing out with training.

5. Keep sessions short; 1 to 2 minutes. Your dog should see the muzzle, consume treats out of it, and be praised. Then remove the muzzle, place it away out of sight and ignore your dog for 1 to 2 minutes.

6. Repeat. Bring the muzzle and treats out and praise your dog for placing his nose in the muzzle. Presence of the muzzle makes you give him treats and attention.

7. Your dog should have several positive experiences over several weeks with the muzzle and treats prior to attaching the neck strap.

8. After your dog is showing excitement when you get the muzzle out and he is readily pushing his nose in the muzzle to eat the treats, you may start placing the strap around the back of his head.

9. Once you have attached the muzzle, you will need to adjust the fit of the neck strap so he is not able to pull if off. Continue to give your dog treats through the basket while he is wearing the muzzle.

Example of a basket muzzle and appropriate treats (hot dog, string cheese, and canned cheese).

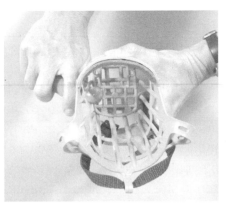

Proper handling: hold the straps back and place a hot dog in the nose of the basket.

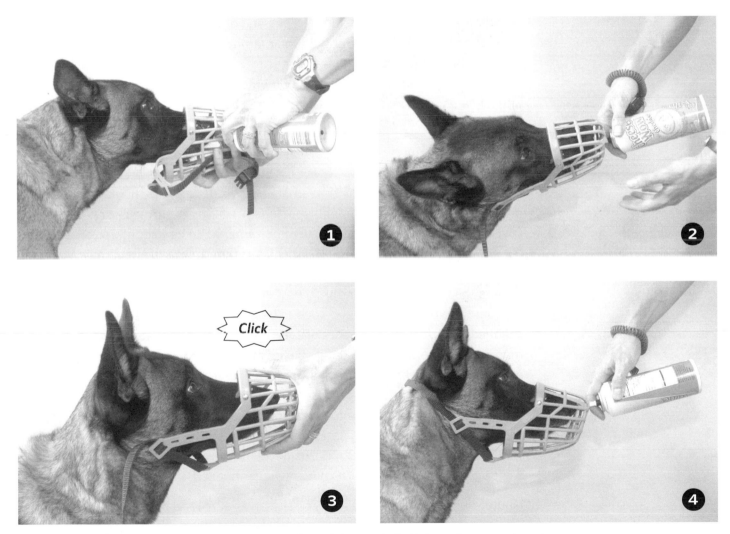

1. Allow your dog to consume canned cheese from the front of the muzzle (hold the neck strap as shown).

2. Progress to presenting the muzzle with the neck strap released.

3. Present the muzzle without treats in it and click when your dog places his nose in the muzzle. Reward (not shown) with a treat through the muzzle.

4. Connect the neck strap and continue to use treats.

# Spay or Neuter?

Gonadectomy (spaying and neutering), the removal of ovaries and uterus or testicles, is one of the most common surgical procedures performed by veterinarians. The procedure is routinely performed on dogs between 6 and 9 months of age or prior to reaching sexual maturity. Early-age spaying and neutering of puppies (as early as 6 to 7 weeks of age) is increasing in popularity. Gonadectomy reduces the risk of unwanted pregnancies resulting in population control of free-roaming dogs. Chances are if your dog is adopted from a shelter, it is already spayed or neutered.

Generally, most pet dogs should be spayed or neutered and not bred. Any intact male or female dog left to their own devices will do what comes natural. There are no behavioral benefits conferred by allowing your dog to have a litter of puppies prior to spaying. Responsible pet parents who own intact dogs need to supervise and manage their dogs to prevent unwanted pregnancies. If breeding your dog, you should be willing and able to take any of the puppies back at any time in their life should their family not be able to care for them. Responsible pet parents and breeders prevent pet overpopulation. The health and behavioral benefits of spaying and neutering generally outweigh the risks and allow us to share our homes with dogs. Discuss the timing of the procedure with your veterinarian.

Intact female dogs cycle biannually and the heat cycle lasts an average of 3 weeks. This corresponds with vaginal bleeding, discharge, and sexual receptivity to males. Spaying the female dog results in many health and behavioral benefits. These benefits include preventing uterine infection (pyometra) and decreasing the risk of mammary cancer or tumors (breast cancer). Mammary tumors are the most common tumor of the female dog (3.4%) and 50% of the time they are malignant. Surgical spaying prior to the first heat cycle results in the lowest chance of mammary cancer (0.5%), compared to between first and second heat cycle (8%), compared to between second heat cycle and 2.5 years of age (26%).[2,3] No reduction in the risk of mammary tumors is suggested if spayed after 2.5 years of age.[4] Aggression associated with a litter of puppies (maternal aggression), a false pregnancy, and heat-induced inter-dog aggression can be avoided by spaying. A disadvantage of spaying female dogs may be an increased risk of developing hormonal-related urinary incontinence. A large study of 983 dogs found that 12.9% of dogs spayed at < 3 months developed urinary incontinence, while only 5% dogs spayed at >3 months became incontinent.[5]

Neutering male dogs offers many health and behavioral benefits. Neutering intact male dogs reduces the incidence of benign prostate enlargement and infection (prostate disease) and perineal hernia, and prevents and reduces perianal adenomas (tumors surrounding the anus).[6] Testicular tumors are common in intact male dogs (incidence of about 1%) and neutering is curative.[7] Behavioral benefits include a decrease in roaming, urine marking, mounting, and fighting. Inter-male aggression is reduced in about one third of dogs. A

**Key points:**

- Most pet dogs should be spayed or neutered.
- The health and behavioral benefits of spaying and neutering generally outweigh the risks.

disadvantage of neutering male dogs is a predisposition to a certain type of cancer. The incidence of prostatic cancer in dogs is approximately 0.05%.[5] Neutered dogs have a higher incidence of developing prostatic cancer than intact dogs, with an increased risk of 2.5 to 5 times.[8]

Spayed and neutered dogs have an increased tendency to develop obesity, yet obesity can be controlled by limiting access to food. The risk of obesity is higher when surgery is performed on sexually mature animals compared to immature animals. Spayed and neutered dogs may be more at risk of developing cognitive dysfunction syndrome (senility or dementia). Dogs that are spayed or neutered before bone growth is complete are taller than intact dogs or dogs that are spayed or neutered at a later age.[9] Orthopedic (bone and joint) diseases in neutered animals are likely to be conditions associated with late or incomplete closure of growth plates or altered joint anatomy due to changes in skeletal growth.[10] Orthopedic conditions may include hip dysplasia, ligament injury of the knee (ACL tear), and fracture of the upper femoral growth plate (slipped capital femoral epiphysis).

**Key points:**

- Discuss with your veterinarian the timing of having your dog spayed or neutered.

- There are advantages and disadvantages to early and late gonadectomy.

- Dogs that are spayed or neutered require fewer calories in order to prevent obesity.

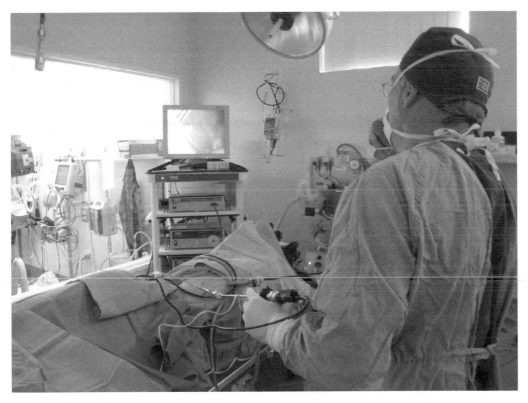

A dog being spayed using laparoscopy. Dogs commonly receive as technologically advanced care as humans.

# Children and Dogs

Growing up with a dog can be good for a child's health and development. A dog in the household has been shown to boost immunity and decrease the risk of allergies or asthma.[11] Studies show that these children have a higher self esteem, improved social skills, and are more popular with their peers. Children who have a family dog tend to have more empathy, be more cooperative, and be more likely to share. Children with pets are more likely to be humane, compassionate, and respectful of all life. A dog in the home provides companionship, trust, love, and responsibility. While we do not want to discourage or deprive children from growing up with dogs, there are some risks that parents should be aware.

Intestinal parasites, such as roundworms and hookworms, are common in puppies and adult dogs and are zoonotic (infectious to humans) through contact with infected feces or soil. Thankfully, good hygiene, common sense, and monthly heartworm/parasite medications can prevent infection. Fleas, ticks, and other topical parasites (scabies) and infections (ringworm) may pose a lesser threat. Year-round monthly prevention with a broad-spectrum parasite product is key. Consult with your veterinarian about preventing these parasites and monitoring and maintaining the health and safety of your family and dog.

The majority of dog bites involve young children and interactions with a familiar or a family dog in the home. The prevalence of dog bites in children is 2.2 % and is double when compared to the general population.[12] The majority of children suffer from facial injuries as the result of dog bites.[13, 14, 15] The average age of children is 5 years, with boys more commonly bitten than girls. A dog well socialized to children is less likely to bite out of fear and aggression. In fact, socialization is the most important thing you can do for your puppy to prevent future dog bites to adults and children.

**Key points:**

- There are many benefits for children growing up with a dog in the home.
- Health risks can be minimized through routine veterinary care and preventative medicine.
- Unfortunately, dog bites involving children are a realistic concern.

Precursors of aggressive behavior, particularly towards children, include:[16, 17]

- Lack of obedience training.

- Little or no socialization with children.

- Aggression over food, toys, and places.

- Being overly sensitive to touch or fearful of people.

- A history of preying on small animals or aggression to family members.

Children should be taught to ask for permission to approach and pet an unfamiliar dog. Dogs should be taught to look to their handler for a treat when being petted by strangers. Treats allow for a positive association with an unfamiliar person.

### Key points:

- Every dog has the potential to bite or show aggression.

- Dogs should not be subjected to inappropriate interactions with children.

- Children can be unpredictable in their interactions with dogs.

- Prevention, management, and teaching appropriate dog interaction skills can minimize risk.

Every dog has the potential to bite or show aggression. For some dogs, the threshold for aggression is lower than others. Medical conditions that result in pain or malaise can reduce tolerance. Even a dog that has been very well socialized can still be provoked to bite, pending the circumstance. Many people have unrealistic expectations of dogs that are uncharacteristic of themselves or other people. Expectations of dogs to never become angry, frightened, irritable, or confrontational at some point are unrealistic. Behaviorally normal dogs will get up and walk away in order to avoid confrontation. Kids don't always get the message and parents should be present to intervene and teach their child what is appropriate. It is unrealistic to believe that all dogs should tolerate inappropriate behavior from children.

Regardless of the level of trust you have in your dog, accidents can happen, because children are unpredictable and don't always think before they behave. Children should be taught to leave dogs alone when resting, sleeping, eliminating, eating, drinking, hiding, or chewing on a bone or toy. Children should avoid approaching any dog behind a barrier such as a fence, baby gate, or when in a kennel. All dogs should be provided with an area of the home in which to retreat that is "off limits" to children. Children should be taught to respect these rules.

Behaviors children should avoid for risk of being bitten:

- Rough play, handling, or petting, including pulling hair, feet, ears, or tail.

- Running or chasing the dog.

- Crawling, climbing, or laying on the dog.

- Reaching to pet unfamiliar or neighborhood dogs.

- Teasing, taunting, growling, or barking at a dog.

- Physical or verbal reprimands.

Throughout interactions, parents should be quick to interrupt undesirable interactions and reward appropriate ones by the dog or child. Hugging or kissing familiar and unfamiliar dogs places children at risk of a facial bite. Hugging and kissing are human affectionate behaviors that many dogs tolerate, but do not enjoy. Fifty-five percent of children suffer post traumatic stress disorder following a substantial bite.[18] Observe your dog for appeasement or conflict behaviors because these signs may be precursors to aggressive behaviors. Care must be taken to monitor your dog's and child's interaction at all times.

Parents expecting to bring a child into the home with their dog should have some concerns over their dog's acceptance of a new baby. Your dog will not know that a baby is human, and the sudden, jerky movements of a baby's limbs combined with crying can over stimulate your dog to play, nip, or bite. Pre-baby counseling prevents and prepares parents and the dog several months in advance of their new arrival. Any parent who has a dog that has shown aggression to children in the home should seek behavioral therapy immediately.

Most children have trouble being consistent and will need parental supervision and intervention. *Living with Kids and Dogs... Without Losing Your Mind*, by Colleen Pelar, CPDT, is a good reference for prevention of problems associated with kids and dogs.

**Key points:**

• Pre-baby counseling prevents and prepares parents and the dog several months in advance of their new arrival.

• Children and dogs should have supervised interactions 100% of the time.

# Multiple Dog Households

Before adding another dog to your household, you should first consider the other animals in your family and whether your living arrangements will accommodate multiple dogs. Your dog's social relationship with another dog will largely depend on the individual personality of each dog. Research the breed of your current dog and your potential new addition to see if they are likely to interact well. Hounds tend to be more accepting of other dogs than terriers, although there are exceptions. It is never a good idea to get two puppies from the same litter for many reasons. Littermates, especially of the same sex, are likely to be close in social rank leading to future sibling rivalry. Littermates kept together tend to bond more strongly with each other than with people. Training is more difficult with two dogs. The monumental task of raising two puppies at the same time is overwhelming for even the most experienced handler.

When picking another companion dog, opposite sex pairs are less likely to fight. Avoid selecting a dog that is close in social stature and age compared to your current dog. A trial period of gradual, supervised interactions is best to make sure the dogs get along.

While living in a multi-dog home can be very rewarding for both people and dogs, you will need to consider how adding another dog will affect the physical and emotional wellness of your current dog or dogs. Visions of your current dog romping with a new friend, playing with each other, and keeping each other company may or may not be realistic. Ask yourself, are you getting another dog because you want one or are you doing it for your current companion? If your answer to the question is one sided, it is best to refrain from a new addition. Dogs that are young and playful are most likely to benefit from a new addition. If your current dog is senior or debilitated, he may be less socially accepting of sharing his space, especially with a vibrant, excitable puppy. Relationships will have to be established and interactions will have to be controlled and managed. Often, in fairness to your current dog, people will have to intervene and teach a pushy puppy what is appropriate through redirection and reward.

Adding another dog can affect your relationship and the care for your current dog. Do you have the time and financial resources to care for an additional pet? Larger dogs are more costly than smaller dogs. Generally, the new dog will monopolize a majority of your attention and time, leaving your current dog feeling left behind or pushed to the periphery. This is especially true when adding a third, fourth, or fifth dog to the household. The more dogs living in the same household, the greater the propensity there is for social stress and competition. At some point, someone is not going to get along. Aggression is more likely when resources become limited or social relationships are changing or unestablished. Some grumbling and groveling may be normal dog communication and allowed, but active fights are damaging to canine social relationships and can negatively affect the human animal bond.

**Key points:**

- Consider your living arrangements and the other animals living in your household prior to adding another dog to the family.

- Avoid adopting two puppies at the same time.

- The more dogs living in the same household, the greater the propensity there is for social stress and competition.

**Key points:**

• Many dogs are accepting of meeting unfamiliar dogs off their property, but it might be different when a new dog moves in permanently.

• Social competition amongst dogs should be minimized through appropriate management.

Many dogs are accepting of meeting unfamiliar dogs off their property, but it might be different when a new dog moves in permanently. Some will enjoy the company of an extra dog in the household, but might still view the other dog as a source of competition. Ask yourself, does your home floor plan accommodate the management of multiple dogs?

In order to minimize social competition, there are some management factors you should initiate in multi-dog households.

These recommendations are important for the prevention of future problems.

• Avoid access to objects that are likely to be guarded when the dogs are in each others presence. These items may include rawhides, pig ears, bones, or chew toys.

• Prevent and/or manage competition over meals by feeding the dogs at set times in different locations of the home. Each dog should have his own bowl and feeding spot. Dinner time can be a time of high arousal. Dogs may be crated prior to preparing meals and fed in their crate.

• Provide separate resting locations (beds) in different areas of the home. Forcing dogs to sleep right next to each other or in the same kennel can lead to future problems. If kennels are used, they should be spaced apart to allow individuality.

• Leash walk the dogs together twice a day off the property. This may only be possible if the dogs are well trained or there is a person to walk each dog. Most dogs enjoy social outings; positive time spent together allows for social bonding between the dogs.

• Train dogs individually each day. A well-trained dog is more relaxed and more easily redirected in any situation.

• Provide behavioral outlets for stress relief. Play games with each dog in a manner that does not cause competition for attention or toys.

Amazingly, many dogs have a remarkable ability to coexist and get along in multi-dog households. A multi-dog household can be rewarding to humans and canine counterparts when managed appropriately. Remember though, social relationships between dogs are not based on equality or democracy. Consistency and predictability of human-dog interactions, training, and training, and a set daily routine will keep the canine family happy and harmonious.

Attention: If you are considering getting another dog, consider pre-purchase counseling in order to prevent future problems. Any dog displaying inter-dog aggression should be evaluated by a qualified behavior professional.

**Key points:**

- Many dogs have a remarkable ability to coexist and get along in multi-dog households.

- Consider pre-purchase counseling in order to prevent future problems when adding another dog to the family.

# Safety and Poison Control

Many common environmental hazards can be prevented by carefully examining the home and yard with a puppy's-eye view. Similar to child proofing your home, you must puppy proof it.

Safeguard any personal or household item that you could not live without; puppies are indiscriminative chewers. Items such as dirty laundry, shoes, and clothing are likely to be chewed and should be stored in their proper place.

Garbage in the trash can, either food based or non food based, can be hazardous. Lidded trash cans are safer than open ones, but they are no substitute for management and supervision. Remember, puppies are opportunistic. Place trash cans in a child-proofed cabinet or behind a closed door.

Objects on low lying furniture such as coffee tables or end tables are likely to be chewed, broken by a tail wag, or knocked over by a puppy exploring the environment. Unstable items or lamps could fall and injure a young puppy. The TV remote control is likely to be chewed if left on the coffee table. Place all cherished knickknacks, decorations, or breakable objects out of reach of your puppy.

Secure all telephone wires, electrical cords, and computer cables. These items are likely to be chewed and pose a risk of electrocution or strangulation. Barricades, plastic cord guards, and commercial taste deterrents may be helpful.

Children's toys, small objects, or office supplies may be chewed or swallowed by a dog. Common office items, such as coins, needles, thread, pens, paper clips, thumbtacks, rubber bands, or staples pose a hazard. Use crates, exercise pens, and baby gates to safeguard your puppy's indoor environment. Earrings and jewelry have been known to be removed and ingested by dogs with exuberant greetings.

Place child locks on all cupboards and cabinets. Household cleaning chemicals pose a hazard. Human over the counter and prescription medicines can be toxic and should be kept out of reach. Dogs will drink out of the toilet and could ingest toilet bowl cleaner unless the lid is kept down. Used bathroom items such as dental floss and feminine hygiene products should be placed in a secure locking trash can or cabinet.

The garage or laundry room may contain cleaners, mothballs, insect poisons, fertilizers, and rodent poisons. These items should be in locking cabinets or stored on high shelves. Antifreeze from a leaking car radiator is a common, fatal poison of dogs. The active ingredient, ethylene glycol, even in small amounts, produces life-threatening kidney damage.

**Key points:**

- Exposure to hazards in the home and yard can be prevented by puppy proofing the environment.

Hazards may be present in your dog's yard. Small rocks or gravel may be ingested. Check the security of fencing surrounding your yard. Look for possible escape routes. Generally, if your puppy's head will fit through the hole or gap, so could the rest of his body. Secure the fence line and supervise your puppy. Block off access to pools or ponds through appropriate fencing or supervise to prevent drowning. Many dogs who have fallen in bodies of water are unable to find their way out safely.

Many plants around the home can be hazardous to your dog. Puppies love to chew, increasing the risk for potential ingestion. Common toxic plants include azalea, rhododendron, philodendron, oleander, castor bean, schefflera, dumb cane, pothos, hydrangea, poinsettia, mistletoe, lily, tulip, narcissus bulbs, amaryllis, yew, morning glory, sago palm, and cactus. Place all potted plants in your home out of reach of your dog. Many plants, trees, and shrubs often used for landscaping or native to the environment can have toxic properties. Survey your dog's yard daily for trees and/or plants that pose potential hazards. Wild mushrooms are extremely toxic if ingested. Supervise your puppy or young dog to prevent accidental ingestion.

**Key points:**

- Puppies should not be left in the yard unsupervised.

- Many common plants can be toxic to dogs.

- Certain everyday human foods can cause vomiting, diarrhea, or even death when consumed by dogs.

**Sago Palm (*Cycas revolute*) contains the toxin, cycasin, with the highest level found in the seeds.**

**All parts of the plant are toxic with a fatality rate of 50 to 75% with ingestion.**

**Signs of ingestion include vomiting, diarrhea, weakness, seizures, liver failure, bleeding, and death.**

Many people are unaware that certain human foods are actually toxic to dogs. Avoid offering your dog chocolate (bakers, semi sweet, milk, dark), grapes, raisins, garlic, onions, certain nuts, foods containing artificial sweeteners, and beverages containing alcohol or caffeine. Unripe green tomatoes and accompanying green leaves and stems are toxic to dogs. Apple seeds, as well as the seeds of peaches, nectarines, plums, etc. can contain cyanide.

The risk of falling is present in multi story residencies with stairs and balconies. Block off access or have your puppy supervised on leash to prevent a fatal fall.

In case of a possible ingestion of a foreign substance or poison, first contact your veterinarian. For all poison-related emergencies or inquires, contact the *Animal Poison Control Center*, 24 hours a day, 365 days a year.

**ASPCA Animal Poison Control Center: (888) 426-4435.**

# References

1.  Association for Pet Obesity Prevention, The National Pet Obesity Day Study. Oct 2009. www.petobesityprevention.com.

2.  Hardie E. Pros and Cons of Neutering. SEVC Proceedings 2007, Southern European Veterinary Conference (Eds). Publisher: SEVC Internet Publisher: International Veterinary Information Service, Ithaca NY (www.ivis.org), Last updated: 21-Oct-2007.

3.  Bergman PJ. Mammary Gland Tumors. *J Natl Cancer Inst* 1983; 70:709–711.

4.  Hardie E. Pros and Cons of Neutering. SEVC Proceedings 2007, Southern European Veterinary Conference (Eds). Publisher: SEVC Internet Publisher: International Veterinary Information Service, Ithaca NY (www.ivis.org), Last updated: 21-Oct-2007.

5.  Okkens AC, Kooistra HS, Nickel RF. Comparison of long term effects of ovariectomy versus ovariohystrectomy in bitches. *J Reprod Fertil Suppl* 1997; 51:227–231.

6.  Hardie E. Pros and Cons of Neutering. SEVC Proceedings 2007, Southern European Veterinary Conference (Eds). Publisher: SEVC Internet Publisher: International Veterinary Information Service, Ithaca NY (www.ivis.org), Last updated: 21-Oct-2007.

7.  Kirpensteijn J. Should we use male castration (orchiectomy) to treat dogs and cats or to prevent disease? Proceedings of the International SCIVAC Congress 2008. International Congress of the Italian Association of Companion Animal Veterinarians, May 30—June 1 2008 Rimini, Italy.

8.  Okkens AC, Kooistra HS, Nickel RF. Comparison of long term effects of ovariectomy versus ovariohystrectomy in bitches. *J Reprod Fertil Suppl* 1997; 51:227–231.

9.  Hardie E. Pros and Cons of Neutering. SEVC Proceedings 2007, Southern European Veterinary Conference (Eds). Publisher: SEVC Internet Publisher: International Veterinary Information Service, Ithaca NY (www.ivis.org), Last updated: 21-Oct-2007.

10. Hardie E. Pros and Cons of Neutering. SEVC Proceedings 2007, Southern European Veterinary Conference (Eds). Publisher: SEVC Internet Publisher: International Veterinary Information Service, Ithaca NY (www.ivis.org), Last updated: 21-Oct-2007.

11. McNicholas, J—University of Warwick, 2002, Ownby DR, Johnson CC, Peterson EL. Exposure to dogs and cats in the first year of life and risk of allergic sensitization at 6 to 7 years of age. *JAMA* 2002; 288: pp 72 to 972.

12. Kahn A, Robert E, Piette D, De Keuster T, Lamoureux J, Leveque A. Prevalence of dog bites in children. A telephone survey. *European J Pediatr* 2004; 163:424.

13. Kahn A, Bauche P, Lamoureux J, and the members of the Dog Bites Research Team. Child victims of dog bites treated in emergency departments. *European J Pediatr* 2003; 162: pp 254-258.

14. Bernardo L, Gardner M, Rosenfield R, Cohen B, Pitetti R. A comparision of dog bite injuries in younger and older children treated in a pediatric emergency department. *Pediatr Emerg Care* 2002 Jun; 18(3): pp 247-249.

15. Schalomon J, Ainoedhofer H, Singer G, Petnehazy T, Mayr J, Kiss K, Hollwarth M. Analysis of dog bites in children who are younger than 17 years. *J Pediatr* 2006 Mar; 117 (3) pp 374–379.

16. Lindsay SR. 2001. *Handbook of Applied Dog Behavior and Training, Volume Two.* Ames: Iowa State University Press.

17. Xavier Manteca, Jaume Fatjó, Marta Amat and Valentina Mariotti. Preventing Canine Aggression: What Works and What Doesn't. Proceeding of the SEVC Southern European Veterinary Conference. Oct. 17-19, 2008—Barcelona, Spain.

18. Peters V, Sottiaux M, Appelboom J, Kahn A. Post traumatic stress disorder after dog bites in children. *J Pediatr* 2004 Jan; 144 (1): pp 17–22.

# CHAPTER 6

# HOUSE TRAINING

## House Training

House training is a term used to describe teaching your dog a "human approved" appropriate elimination area. Usually, this location is outdoors on grass, but dogs can be litter-box trained or trained to eliminate on other surfaces such as concrete. Elimination training, or teaching your dog to eliminate in appropriate locations, is the most important behavior for the indoor dog in terms of owner retention. Dogs are often relinquished to shelters due to lack of house training.

Successful elimination training depends on your ability to effectively communicate to your puppy where you consider it appropriate for him to eliminate. This process will not occur overnight. Punishment, including verbal reprimands, only teaches your dog not to eliminate in front of you, making house training very difficult.

> Prevention of accidents through management and supervision is the key to successful house training.

**Key points:**

- House training is an important behavioral concept for the indoor dog.
- Similar to potty training a toddler, your puppy will not be house trained overnight.
- Prevention of accidents through management and supervision is necessary for success.
- Surface preferences are established early in life.

Dogs are unlikely to eliminate in areas where they eat or sleep making the use of a crate ideal for prevention and management.

Grass is a preferable substrate for elimination only if a puppy has had exposure and has been rewarded for elimination on the surface at an early age.

## Surface Preference

Surface or substrate preferences are established early in life, usually during the socialization period. A dog's natural preference is to eliminate on porous surfaces, in a place where elimination has previously occurred, and away from his eating and sleeping areas.

# 5 Steps to Successful House Training

## *1. Prevent Accidents from Occurring*

• In general, when not engaged in physical activity, a puppy can hold his urine for 1 hour plus his age in months. For example, a 3-month-old puppy should be able to hold it for 4 hours when not active. Maximum duration of urine retention should not exceed 8 hours for any dog greater than 7 months of age. Full bladder control may take 4 to 5 months to develop, but accidents may occasionally occur up to 1 year of age. Similarly, potty training toddlers is a developmental process that will vary with each individual.

• Direct supervision is imperative. Use the umbilical cord technique whereby your puppy is attached to you with a leash. Tethering the dog to you with a leash improves supervision. If you are unable to give your puppy your full attention, such as when you are cooking, talking on the phone, or otherwise preoccupied, confine him to a small area or crate.

• Crates can make elimination training much easier because if acclimated properly to the crate, most puppies will accept the crate as a comforting and secure place. Feeding meals in the crate or the confinement area makes entering and occupying the space rewarding.

• If your confinement area is too large, your puppy might eliminate in one area and sleep in another area. When used for housetraining, crates should only be large enough for the dog to lie down, stand up, and turn around. You may have to barricade a portion of a large crate in order to reduce the size.

• Never use the crate or confinement area as a punishment.

• Feed a consistent, highly digestible diet at set times 2 to 3 times a day. Allow your puppy 20 minutes to eat his meal and then remove the food bowl. Do not offer food 2 hours prior to bedtime to help insure success through the night.

• Water should be freely available to your puppy at all times. Restricting water induces excessive water consumption when offered. Consequently, excessive and frequent urination will follow.

## 2. Reward Elimination in Appropriate Areas

- Use a cue phrase, such as "Let's go outside" or "Outside."

- Use the same exit from the house and take the dog out on a leash every time (even if you have a fenced-in yard). Designate a specific area of the yard for elimination.

- Withhold attention from him until he eliminates. This means do not talk to, play with, or look at him.

- Add a cue phrase, such as "Hurry up" just prior to elimination. This allows you to get elimination behavior on cue.

- Praise your dog with attention *after* he eliminates and offer a treat. If in a securely fenced area, you can reward with off-lead playtime.

- If he does not go, take him inside and supervise or confine him and then try again in 10 to 15 minutes.

> **Key points:**
> - Your puppy's elimination routine should be consistent.
> - Cue your dog to go potty and reward him for eliminating in appropriate locations.
> - Anticipate when your puppy will need to eliminate.
> - Keep a log of elimination, activity, and feeding in order to learn your puppy's routine.

## 3. Anticipate when your Puppy Needs to Eliminate

- Set your puppy up to succeed by anticipating when he will need to eliminate.

- Keep a log of elimination, activity, and feeding in order to learn your puppy's routine. Know when your puppy is full or empty.

- Make repeated trips. First thing in the morning, last thing at night, and several times in between.

- Take a potty break after eating, playing, and sleeping. Your puppy is likely to eliminate after finishing one behavior and before beginning another.

- During the day, while you are home, you should take your dog outside frequently, whether you think he needs to eliminate or not. When indoors, confine him if you are unable to supervise. This will set him up to succeed.

- Watch for your puppy's signals of impending elimination: sniffing the ground, wandering to the door, circling.

> An initial examination by a veterinarian is important to rule out medical factors contributing to house soiling. Medical disorders, such as urinary tract infection or vaginitis in females, are not uncommon in puppies. Any concurrent medical disorder that increases the frequency of urination or defecation may make house training impossible. Any regression in house training may indicate a visit to the veterinarian is necessary.

## 4. When Accidents Happen

- Do not punish your dog for house soiling. Yelling at or scolding your puppy for accidents will only teach him to be afraid and not eliminate in front of you. This makes house training difficult. Punishment does not teach your puppy where it is appropriate to eliminate.

- If your puppy is having an accident, use the cue, "Outside," to interrupt the behavior and teach him to go outdoors. This may momentarily make him stop and give you the opportunity to take him outside and praise him for eliminating in the proper location.

**Key points:**

- Punishment does not teach your puppy where it is appropriate to eliminate.

- Accidents should be handled through redirection.

- Clean soiled areas appropriately to prevent future accidents in the same location.

## 5. Cleaning Soiled Areas

- Because dogs will be drawn to spots where elimination has previously occurred, it is extremely important to thoroughly clean soiled areas to prevent further accidents.

- Avoid applying any cleaning products that contain ammonia, vinegar, or bleach. These may actually attract your puppy back to the area.

- Hard surfaces should first be cleaned with an enzymatic cleaner. Allow the area to dry and then apply a pine- or lemon-scented product.

- Carpets should be cleaned with an enzymatic cleaner designed for eliminating pet odors. Allow the area to dry for 24 hours. Apply 1/8 of a teaspoon of finely crushed mothballs to the area. Brush the powder deep into the pile of the carpet or fabric so that none is exposed. Mothball crystals make the area locally aversive. You should not be able to smell the mothballs when you enter the room or sniff the carpet a few feet away. Reapply weekly for a month.

- CAUTION: Mothball crystals are toxic to dogs and people if consumed. It is unlikely for your puppy to ingest previously soiled carpet/fabric containing mothball crystals. Do not use mothball crystals on bedding, in areas where the puppy is confined, or on objects that may be chewed or ingested.

**Using these techniques, most puppies can be successfully house trained. To be effective, however, all steps must be followed simultaneously and consistently.**

# Forced to leave your puppy for extended periods of time?

If you are forced to leave your puppy for extended periods of time, provide him with an appropriate elimination location within a larger confinement area. The elimination area should be separate from sleeping and eating areas. Consider using an exercise pen, a large crate, or a small room. Alternatively, hire a dog walker to provide your puppy opportunities to eliminate outdoors.

When the ultimate goal is for your puppy to eliminate outside on grass, we recommend using sod in a dog litter box located in the confinement area. Alternatives to sod include dog litter, newspaper, or pee pads in the litter box. Initially, take your puppy to the litter box on leash and reward him at the end of the elimination with praise and a treat. This teaches him that the litter box is an appropriate location for elimination. The presence of urine or stool in the litter box may be used to attract your puppy to eliminate in the box.

The disadvantage of using pee pads or paper training indoors is that it is an extra step to fade in order to reach the ultimate goal of eliminating outdoors. Your puppy may develop a preference for urinating/defecating on objects located on the floor, such as bath mats, throw rugs, clothing, towels, door mats, or paper. Using a litter box and sod minimizes accidents just off the paper or pad and problematic associations with other similar porous substrates.

### Key points:

- Provide your puppy an appropriate elimination location indoors when left at home alone for extended periods of time.

- Use a litter box as an indoor alternative rather than placing pee pads or paper directly on the floor.

- Using sod in the litter box teaches an appropriate surface preference.

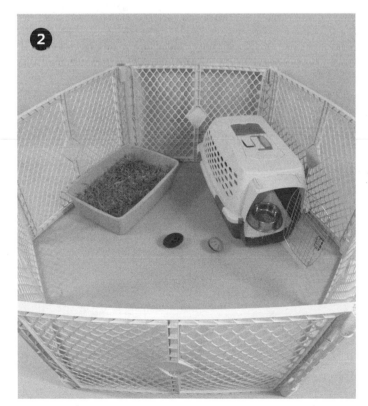

1. Grass sod placed in a large litter box provides a suitable substrate for elimination.

2. An exercise pen provides an area for eating, sleeping, play, and elimination.

# Other Reasons for Inappropriate Elimination

## *Marking*

Marking with urine, or leg-lifting behavior, is often an anxiety related behavioral disorder that is unrelated to house training. It is a behavioral outlet of stressed dogs and a form of territorial communication. The behavior may coincide with puberty or begin at 6 months of age. It is most common in sexually mature male dogs, but it may also occur in neutered males. Intact or spayed females rarely mark their territory with urine. Marking behavior is influenced by the presence of testosterone, and surgical neutering may reduce the frequency by 50 to 60 percent. If your dog is marking or leg lifting in unacceptable locations, see your veterinarian or a veterinary behaviorist. Most cases of urine marking dramatically improve with veterinary behavioral therapy.

**Key points:**

- Marking with urine is an anxiety-related behavior that is unrelated to knowing where it is appropriate to eliminate.

- Young dogs may urinate out of excitement associated with incomplete bladder control.

A male dog urine marking on the bushes.

## *Excitement Urination*

Excitement urination often occurs in young puppies and adolescent dogs with over exuberant greetings toward people and dogs. The puppy may be jumping up to greet you or running wildly and urinating at the same time. As urinary sphincter tone increases with maturity, many dogs outgrow the condition. Some adult dogs will continue to urinate when overly excited. The behavior is unrelated to house training. Preventing excitement by making arrivals and greetings low key usually improves the behavior. Veterinary behavioral therapy should be considered for treatment when the behavior is problematic.

## *Submissive Urination*

Submissive urination is a normal behavior and can occur in dogs at any age. It is a fear reaction to a perceived threat and is unrelated to house training. The behavior may be related to underdeveloped urinary sphincter tone in puppies. It is not associated with incontinence seen in older dogs or spayed females. When submissive urination is excessive, these puppies or dogs are uncertain, fearful, or appeasing when greeting unfamiliar people and/or dogs. The dog may squat down, turn slightly to the side, or even roll over while urinating. He is attempting to communicate non-threat and appeasement. Direct eye contact, as well as leaning over, reaching for, or scolding the dog may induce the behavior.

Cases related to sphincter tone improve with maturity and/or concurrent veterinary-prescribed medications. The behavior may improve as the dog's confidence increases. Positive-based training using food treats boosts confidence, allows for positive associations with people, and provides consistent human-dog interactions. Any form of punishment is counterproductive. Avoid threatening body language, including direct eye contact and leaning over or reaching for the dog. Consult with your veterinarian about further treatment or seek a referral to a veterinary behaviorist. Most cases greatly improve with veterinary behavioral therapy.

**Key points:**

- Submissive urination is a normal appeasement behavior of dogs to avoid confrontation.

Scruffles is rolling over and urinating submissively with the approach of a person.

# INTRODUCTION TO TRAINING

## Introduction

Dogs that receive basic training are at a reduced risk for relinquishment.[1] Living with an untrained dog is equally stressful for the dog, as well as his human companion. Imagine being placed into a novel environment where people are attempting to communicate with you in a complicated and foreign language. While trying to learn a new skill, people are speaking to you in gibberish, making it difficult to concentrate. Unfortunately, this is the life of many dogs. It is through foundation training and teaching your dog verbal cues that you and your dog will begin to develop a fluent line of communication. Our positive approach to foundation training makes learning a fun game for you and your dog. This chapter will teach you how to train your dog to respond to verbal cues, thereby improving communication, your social relationship, and the quality of life for you and your dog.

## Intonation

Use a happy and upbeat tone of voice when training your dog. Many dogs find verbal praise reinforcing. Dogs have a very astute sense of hearing. Using a threatening or harsh tone of voice is not fun for you or your dog. If you teach with a stern voice, your dog will only listen when you are stern. You do not want a relationship with your dog based on fear. Always deliver cues in a soft, positive tone. This teaches him to pay attention and listen for the cue, and makes learning enjoyable.

**Key points:**

- Proper training is important for your dog's physical and emotional well-being.
- Training should be fun for you and your dog.
- Use a soft, positive, and upbeat tone of voice when training your dog.

## Motivation

In order for your dog to want to work for you, he must be motivated. Motivation should come from the opportunity for your dog to obtain a reward. To motivate your dog, you must possess something that he desires. Your dog must anticipate that he will get something he finds rewarding. Motivation may come in the form of a treat, a toy, an opportunity to perform a desired behavior, or praise.

Most people would not be willing to work for free. However, many people expect that their dogs should just want to please, or should work for praise alone. These assumptions are unrealistic. People require positive reinforcement through a pat on the back, a paycheck, or even better, a bonus. Most people would be unwilling to work for verbal encouragement alone, and dogs are no different. Although you may enjoy what you do for a living, if suddenly you were no longer compensated or appreciated, you might start to look for a new job. Our relationship with dogs is a social one, and dogs, like people, learn best through positive reinforcement. You must compensate your dog for a job well done.

## Rewards

Rewards that are most commonly used in training include food (treats) or toys. While some dogs with a high working drive enjoy fetching a ball or a game of tug greater than the desire for a treat, there are some initial benefits to training with treats. Readily consumable treats allow for a rapid rate of reinforcement in a short period of time. Without the down time of tossing, retrieving, and relinquishing the toy in a training session, repetitions are maximized. This allows dogs to learn faster. Therefore, dogs should start training with food. Fortunately, because you control when and how much you feed your dog, training with food rewards will not make your dog obese. Training should occur when your dog is hungry. There is no such thing as a healthy puppy or dog who is relaxed that is unmotivated by treats. As training progresses and as your dog learns to bring and relinquish a toy, toys should be incorporated as reinforcement.

Food and toys should be utilized as rewards to keep your dog motivated when training.

# Markers: Conditioned Reinforcers

Training with markers is a way of communicating with your dog using operant and classical conditioning. A marker is a "bridging stimulus" that identifies to your dog that a behavior will receive reinforcement. I think of the marker as taking a picture of your dog's behavior and freezing the behavior in time. Behaviors can be marked the instant they occur. This precise timing expedites learning. A behavior that is marked can be reinforced. A behavior that is reinforced increases in frequency. A marker tells your dog, "That's it! That is the behavior that earned you a reward." When your dog does a behavior and hears the marker, he knows he has done the correct behavior, and anticipates positive reinforcement. Markers allow you to reinforce behaviors when your dog is working at a distance. Use markers; it's the best way to train!

## Types of Markers

A marker can be anything that indicates to your dog that it will receive reinforcement. Examples of markers include a clicker, word, whistle, or flash of light. The ideal marker is a unique or distinct indicator of positive reinforcement. The marker must always be paired with reinforcement for it to maintain its meaning and positive predictive value.

### Clicker

A clicker is a handheld acoustic device that makes a sharp "click" sound. Once the dog has become conditioned to the clicker, the click tells your dog it has done the correct behavior and reinforcement (treat) is coming. Because the clicker is a unique and novel sound, it is a very desirable marker.

### Verbal Marker

A verbal marker is a spoken word. The ideal word is one syllable. It should be novel and not used much in everyday speech. A commonly used verbal marker is the word "Yes."

Dogs learn 45% faster when initially trained new behaviors with a clicker, rather than the use of a verbal marker.[1] Reasons may include the fact that the clicker is a novel stimuli that only means one thing (a treat is coming) compared to human words which tend to be "tuned out" by dogs. *The clicker is the desired marker for training new behaviors.* We advise you to start training your dog with the clicker for this reason.

Once your dog has learned behavioral responses that are on cue, transitioning to a verbal marker may be accomplished. Verbal markers have the benefit of eliciting social interactions and because dogs are social, looking and talking to your dog may be reinforcing. Talking to your dog when he is trying to learn a new behavior or a new cue can be very distracting. Refrain from verbally distracting your dog when initially teaching a new behavior.

**Key points:**

- A marker is a bridge that identifies to your dog when he has preformed the correct behavior and will receive reinforcement.
- The ideal marker is succinct, unique, and clear to your dog.
- The clicker is the desired marker for training new behaviors.

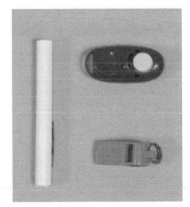

Examples of markers: clicker, whistle, pen light

# Training Tools

## *Clicker*

There are a variety of clickers commercially available. We recommend attaching the clicker to a wrist coil (commonly used for keys). This makes it easily accessible and allows the clicker to remain hidden in your hand.

Wrist coil and clicker

Types of clickers (left to right): standard box clicker, Karen Pryor i-Click, StarMark Clicker, Clicker+ (digital finger clicker), Premier Clik-R (finger Clik-R), whistle clicker.

## *Treats and Treat Bag*

Treats should be small, highly palatable, and readily consumed. Size should be approximately that of a pea or a Cheerio. Your dog ingests them easily and immediately wants another without becoming full. Using a variety of treats of varying value keeps your dog motivated. In non-distracting environments, lower value treats should be used. Save your dog's favorite treats for distracting environments.

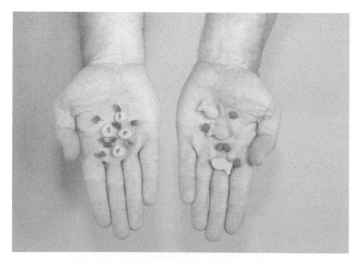

A variety of appropriate-size treats: liver biscotti, Cheerios, dog food kibble, Goldfish crackers.

Delivery of soft food: canned cheese, washable squeeze tubes for delivery of a lick of canned dog food or peanut butter.

| COMMONLY USED TREATS | | | | |
|---|---|---|---|---|
| Dry Dog Food | Canned Dog Food | Commercial Treats | Cereal/Cheerios | Popcorn |
| Hot Dogs | Cooked Boneless Chicken/Turkey | Lunch Meat | Cubed Ham | Goldfish Crackers |
| String Cheese | Canned Easy Cheese | Peanut Butter | Cooked Pasta | Fruits/Vegetables |

The list of training treats is endless. Find what your dog likes and use it. Variety is important. Treats should not make up more than 10% of your dog's caloric intake. Using treats in training will not make your dog overweight. Overfeeding your dog will. In non-distracting environments, use your dog's regular dog food. You may decrease your dog's regular feedings in order to compensate for using treats.

A treat bag, fanny pack, canvas tool apron, or training jacket makes treats easily accessible. No fumbling in your pocket, dropping treats, or your dog stealing a baggy full of treats off the counter!

**Do Not Feed Your Dog:**

- Chocolate
- Grapes
- Raisins
- Meat bones
- Foods with artificial sweeteners, caffeine, or alcohol
- Avocados
- Garlic
- Onions
- Macadamia nuts

Training jacket: deep pockets front and back allow for ample tugs, toys, and food treats.

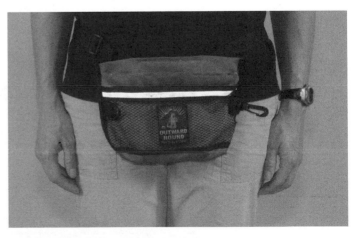

Treat bag: allows for easily accessible treats.

## Collar and Leash

When training outside in a non-fenced area, your dog should be on a leash (lunge line) for safety. Most cities have a leash law requiring dogs to be leashed in public areas. Use a 5 to 10 foot leather or nylon leash with a flat leather or nylon collar, harness, or head collar. Collars might loosen. Check the fit of your dog's collar every time you attach the leash. The collar should fit snugly to avoid your dog getting loose. We do not recommend choke collars, pinch/prong collars, or remote/electric collars for teaching new behaviors.

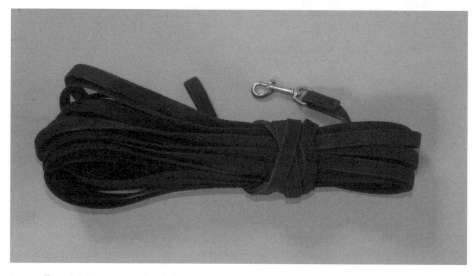

**Lunge line:** 30-foot cotton leash for training at a distance from your dog.

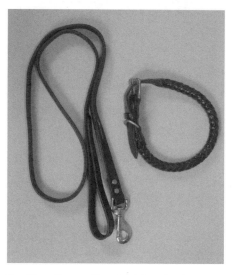

**Buckle collar and leash:** 6-foot leather leash and adjustable leather buckle collar.

## Target Stick

You will use a target stick to train a variety of behaviors. Commercially produced target sticks are available, but a ruler, pen, spatula, or wooden spoon will work.

Examples of Target Sticks:

• Karen Pryor's extendable target stick

• Homemade wooden dowel

• Premier's Terry Ryan extendable target stick with built-in clicker

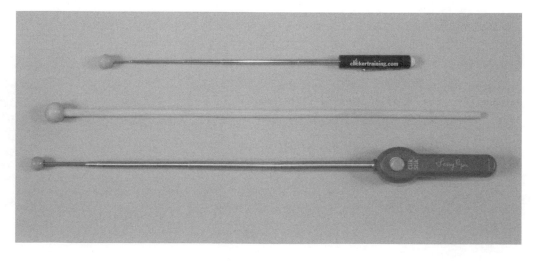

# Training Methods

*Capturing* refers to marking and reinforcing behaviors your dog offers spontaneously.

With capturing, the teacher must only observe a behavior, mark, and reinforce. You may be sitting on the couch and you observe your dog lying down. All you have to do is click when you see him lying down and toss a reward. Reinforced behaviors will increase in frequency.

Capturing is a hands-off form of training commonly used in zoo animals. No prompts or lures are used. Your dog has to think of what he did in order to earn the click and treat. Capturing allows you to place a behavior on cue that the dog performs naturally, such as sitting, lying down, blinking, sneezing, or licking his lips. When the behavior is predictable, it is placed on cue.

**Key points:**

- Training your dog may be accomplished through capturing and shaping.

- With capturing and shaping, your dog is an active participant in learning.

**Shaping:** Iliana's behavior has been shaped to the goal of settling on her bed in a down position.

*Shaping* refers to capturing small progressive steps toward the goal behavior.

Shaping is used to teach more complex behaviors that might not occur spontaneously. When shaping you must have a mental picture of the goal behavior you wish to train. Small steps in the direction of your final goal behavior are reinforced. You might use shaping to teach your dog to go and settle on his bed in a down position. Initially, you may click him for looking at his bed, or taking a step in that direction, and then reward. Progressively, you would hold out or delay the click until he touches the bed with his paw. With shaping, the criteria for reinforcement are changing in steps toward the goal behavior. Once your dog is reliably offering a resemblance of the goal behavior, the cue is added.

When capturing and shaping, you must be patient. Initially, it may be frustrating if your dog is used to you giving him direction. Behaviors taught through capturing and shaping are retained and do not require the fading of a prompt or lure. Capturing and shaping are preferable methods of training.

When you were a kid, you probably remember being told at one time or another, "You will learn it better if you figure it out on your own." When not knowing how to spell a word, if you looked it up in the dictionary, you were more likely to remember the spelling next time. However, if you use spell check on the computer, or ask someone else how to spell the word, it is less likely to be remembered.

Capturing and shaping allow your dog to think about what he is doing in order to earn the mark and reward. Your dog will remember a behavior better when he is actively thinking rather than simply following a treat or target.

**Targeting** refers to teaching your dog to touch his nose, paw, or some other body part to your hand or another object.

Once your dog knows how to target, you can use targeting to prompt and teach many new behaviors. These behaviors may include sit, down, and loose leash walking. Your dog has to think about touching a part of his body to the target in order to receive a click and treat. Targets are easier to fade than food lures and require more of a cognitive component from your dog. Your dog has to touch the target prior to the presentation of a food reward. He is thinking and learning rather than just following a food treat in your hand.

**Key points:**

• Capturing and shaping are preferable methods of training because they do not require the fading of lures or prompts.

• Targeting refers to teaching your dog to touch a body part to an object.

• Targeting is helpful in teaching a variety of behaviors.

Examples of Targeting:

**1.** Iris is targeting a stick with her nose.

**2.** Iris is targeting a hand with her paw.

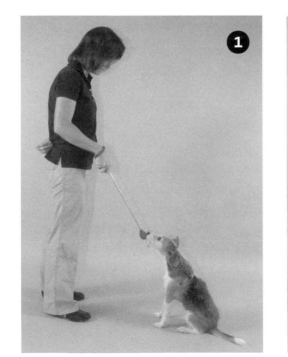

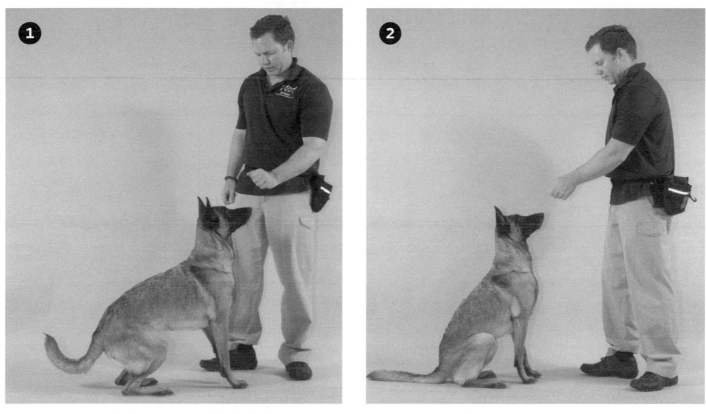

**Example of Luring: 1. & 2.** Iliana is lured to sit with a treat in the handler's hand.

Luring refers to using a food treat to "lure" your dog to perform a desired behavior.

Luring is a form of targeting whereby the dog follows the treat instead of a target. A treat is held in your hand in front of your dog's nose and as your dog follows the treat, you lure him into a position and click and treat. Like a fish following a lure, where his head goes, his body follows.

Many dogs will become too focused on the treat and, therefore, will be unaware of what what their bodies are doing. When luring is used often, it can become difficult to fade the treat out of training. Ideally, fading of the treat should occur as soon as possible (after a few repetitions). This results in targeting, which is preferable. When training a new behavior in distracting environments, luring may be necessary to keep your dog focused.

Consider the analogy of driving to an unfamiliar destination. When following another vehicle to the location, you are less inclined to take notice of landmarks or street names. Finding the location again on your own may prove difficult. If you use a GPS guidance system, you are likely to pay a little more attention to landmarks, but in the future it would still be difficult to navigate to the same location without guidance. In contrast, using a map and planning the necessary steps to arrive at the final destination will help you remember the entire process.

**Key points:**

- Luring is a form of targeting where your dog is following a treat.

- The fading of the treat in hand should occur as soon as possible; this results in targeting.

- Luring is the least preferable method of training because the dog often becomes fixated on the hand holding the treat.

## Clicker Mechanics

We recommend that you first practice clicking and delivering treats without your dog. The mechanics of clicking and treating are extremely important. You will first need to be comfortable with handling the clicker and treats before you are ready to train your dog.

If possible, use a video camera to record your sessions, so you can watch your mechanics and see what your dog will see.

**Key points:**

- Practice your clicker mechanics prior to training your dog.
- Use a mirror or video recording device to perfect your mechanics.

What you will need: 20 pieces of your dog's dry dog food in a treat bag, your clicker, and a plastic cup.

- Place the cup on a table and stand in front of it (the cup is your dog for this exercise).

- Put about 5 to 6 pieces of kibble in your left hand.

- Place your clicker in your right hand with your thumb positioned to click.

- Hold both hands at your side.

- Press the clicker one time and release. Keep your clicker hand at your side—it is not a remote control, so try not to point it towards your dog when training.

- *After the click is complete*, move your left hand towards the cup and drop one piece of kibble into the cup.

- Return your left hand to your side

- As soon as your left hand returns to your side, press the clicker again.

- Repeat until all 20 treats are in the cup.

The first time you perform this exercise, concentrate on keeping your treat hand still until after the click is complete. Do not worry about how quickly you are performing the exercise. It is extremely important that the delivery of the treat begins after the click. If the treat is moving toward the dog or you are reaching into your treat bag while you click, the sound of the clicker will not be significant. The relevant information to him will be the movement of the treat hand.

As you become more comfortable, try to increase your pace, so there is no lag time from the completion of the click and the beginning of the treat delivery. Your dog will need you to be quick with the delivery of the treat in order for him to learn the association between the click and the treat.

Your clicker may be held in either hand. For simplicity, exercises will be described based on the clicker being in the right hand unless otherwise stated.

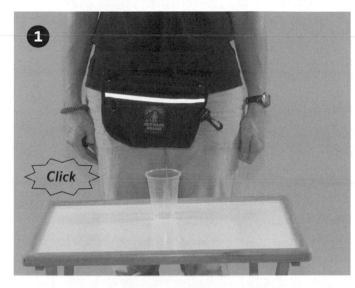

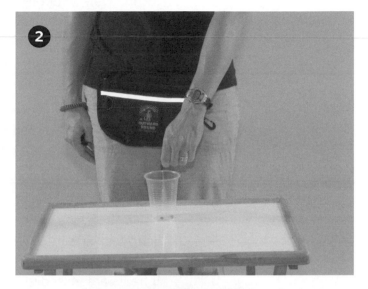

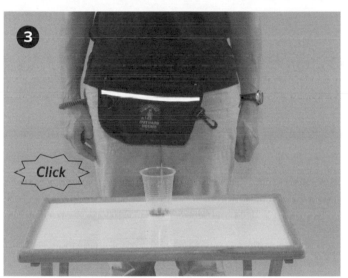

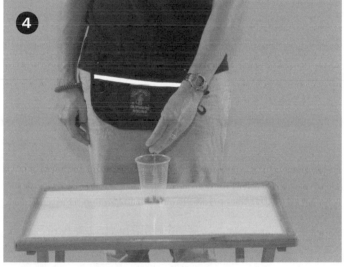

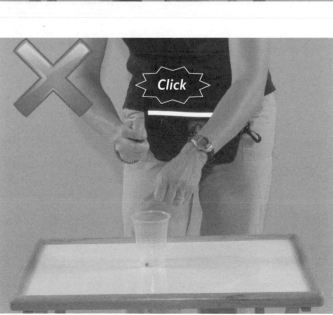

1. **Clicker and treat hand are held at side.**

2. **After completion of the click, deliver the treat.**

3. **Click when hands are back at side.**

4. **After completion of the click, deliver the treat.**

✖ **Incorrect form.**

Notice the treat hand is moving during the click. The clicker is being pointed at the dog. Patterned movement preceding the click will become the cue to your dog.

## Treat Delivery

Instinctively, your dog's head and eyes will drift toward the hand or location of the treat delivery. Variety is important. The treat should sometimes be delivered from the right hand, left hand, or even from your mouth. Vary the location of your treat bag and the treat delivery location relative to your body: from your side, your midline, etc.

Drifting toward the treat can be used to our advantage, rewarding the dog in a specific location or body position. When teaching stationary cues or a duration behavior (a sit-stay or down-stay), it can be helpful to reward your dog in the position you wish him to maintain. Returning and rewarding your dog in position teaches him to stay put.

Other times, we will recommend you toss the treat on the ground away from your dog. Tossing the treat makes your dog move and resets him to perform the behavior again. When tossing the treat, vary the location in relation to your dog. If treats are tossed too often, your dog may look to the floor for treats.

If your dog grabs your entire hand when taking the treat, avoid pulling your hand away. This may inadvertently teach him to grab even harder before the treat disappears. When dogs are nervous, they may take treats rougher. Simply hold your hand still until your dog softens his mouth and then release the treat. A pair of soft leather gloves may be used to protect your skin when using this method.

Once you are comfortable with clicking and treating, it is time to teach your dog the meaning of the clicker!

### Key points:

- Vary the location of your treat bag with each training session.
- Vary treat delivery from each hand and occasionally your mouth.
- Tossing the treat away from your dog is helpful to reset him for doing the behavior again.
- Avoid pulling your hand away when your dog reaches for the treat; pulling the treat briskly away only teaches him to be more grabby.

1. Example of the treat bag worn on the back in order to prevent fixation on the treat bag.

2. Rewarding the down position by offering treats between the forepaws helps with anticipation and Iliana maintaining the position.

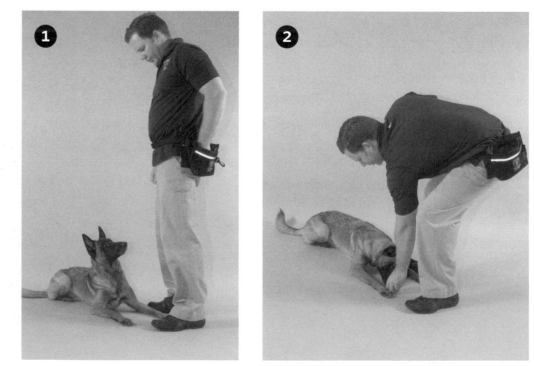

# Conditioning the Clicker

What you will need:

- Hungry dog

- Clicker

- 30 to 40 small treats in a treat bag

- Quiet non-distracting environment

Get yourself ready with 5 to 6 treats in your left hand and your clicker in your right hand. Keep your hands at your side or behind your back. Remember the mechanics of clicking and treating: treat hand moves after the click is complete.

The first time you click, make sure your dog is not right next to the clicker. The sound may startle some dogs at first. This is usually short lived. To avoid a problem, muffle the clicker by placing it behind your back or in your pocket.

Click > Give your dog a treat. Repeat 10 times.

Click > Toss the treat on the ground. Repeat 10 times.

Change your body position > Click > Give your dog a treat. Repeat 10 times.

**Key points:**

- Conditioning the clicker teaches your dog the significance of the marker.

- Muffle the sound of the clicker by initially placing it behind your back on in your pocket.

- Vary your body posture and treat delivery.

- The clicker is conditioned when, after clicking, your dog turns to you in anticipation of a food treat.

Varying your body position when clicking prevents your dog from fixating on your body language. You should sometimes be moving and sometimes standing still when clicking.

Vary the method of treat delivery: deliver it from your left or right hand, toss it on the ground, or spit it from your mouth. Vary the location of your treat bag: in front, at your side, or behind your back. This prevents your dog from becoming fixated on the source of the treat.

Right now you are not asking your dog to perform a specific behavior. He is simply learning that when he hears the click a treat will follow. Dogs quickly learn the association of the marker paired with the delivery of a reward. Conditioning the clicker may be accomplished in as little as 20 to 30 pairings.

## Cues

Cues can be anything the dog can perceive: auditory, visual, tactile, olfactory (smell), environmental (contextual), or even gustatory (taste). The most common cues taught to dogs are audible and visual cues. Auditory cues include words ("Sit," "Down," "Heel," "Come") and sounds (whistle, bell). Hand signals are an example of visual cues. If using luring or targeting to teach a behavior, your hand or finger movement can be a visual cue.

In general, it is easier for your dog to learn a visual cue than an auditory cue. Dogs are in tune with our body language. Because people are verbally oriented, most of our cues are verbal ones.

A sequence of training may go as follows: give the cue, dog performs the behavior, click to mark the behavior, and reinforce with a treat. When cues are consistently followed by positive reinforcement, the cue alone can become a reinforcer of a preceding behavior.

**Key points:**

- Give your audible cue just prior to any body motion if using luring or targeting, otherwise, your dog will only learn your body language (the visual cue).

- Avoid saying your dog's name prior to cueing a behavior.

- Give verbal cues in a upbeat tone of voice.

- Avoid excessive talking to your dog or repeating the verbal cue over and over when training; it is distracting and offers no additional information.

### Characteristics of a good verbal cue:

- One word, instead of a phrase or sentence.

- "Bed" rather than "Go to your bed."

- 1 to 2 syllables.

- Unique and sounding different from each other or your dog's name.

- Words that are not commonly used in everyday conversation.

- Delivered in an upbeat tone rather than a threatening one.

## Adding the Cue

The cue is added once you are able to predict that your dog will perform the desired behavior. A cue is taught after your dog understands the behavior. Give the cue prior to the behavior. Your dog should be reliably offering the behavior before you add the cue.

It is easy to talk too much to your dog when training, causing the verbal cue to get lost in the verbiage. If you were trying to figure out a crossword puzzle and someone kept talking to you, you would lose your train of thought. Excessive talking slows learning because it distracts your dog when trying to learn. It is ok to use verbal praise after completion of a behavior. Avoid verbal encouragement to induce a behavior.

There is no need to continuously repeat the verbal cue over and over. Saying it more than once or louder does not make your dog learn the word faster. Practice giving your verbal cues in a soft, positive tone.

Once you have added the cue, you will allow your dog to occasionally offer the behavior prior to giving him the cue. These non-cued behaviors will not be rewarded. Your dog will learn the relevance of the cue.

**Example of adding the cue for sitting once it is predictable:**

**1.** Dog offers the sit. Click and treat (CT).

**2A & 2B.** Just before the dog begins to sit, give the verbal cue, "Sit." CT when he sits, repeat 20 times.

**3.** Pause for a second and *do not* give the sit cue. If your dog waits for the cue, cue him and CT. If he offers a sit without the cue, do not CT.

**4A & 4B.** Reset your dog by taking a few steps away; give the "Sit" cue. CT when he sits, repeat 20 times.

## Stimulus Control

A cue is considered under stimulus control when (in a training session) your dog:

- Offers the behavior in response to the cue at least 80% of the time.

- Does not offer the behavior in response to another cue.

- Does not offer a different behavior in response to the cue.

## Fluency

When training dogs, we should strive for fluency. Think about being fluent in a foreign language; you must be able to understand, pronounce, write and read the words, and use the words smoothly in conversation. Fluency will not occur overnight, whether training dogs or learning a foreign language.

**Criteria for a fluent behavior include:**
- Stimulus control.

- Precision: the behavior is polished and precise.

- Low latency: your dog begins to perform the behavior quickly in response to the cue.

- Speed: your dog performs the behavior as fast as possible.

- The 3 **D**s: your dog will perform the behavior under **Distraction, with Duration, and at a Distance.**

## Schedules of Reinforcement

Schedules of reinforcement are the rules that determine if a behavior will be followed by reinforcement or reward. These rules are stated in terms of the time between reinforcement and/or the number of behavioral responses required to receive reinforcement. Think about reinforcement schedules in terms of when and how often you will offer your dog a treat or toy for performing a behavior in a training session.

### *Continuous Reinforcement (CRF)*

The desired behavioral response is reinforced every single time it occurs with a continuous reinforcement schedule. For example, in a training session using continuous and positive reinforcement, every time your dog sits you offer a treat. Continuous reinforcement is best used during the initial stages of learning in order to build a strong association between the behavior and the response. Continuous reinforcement expedites and solidifies the learning of new behaviors. Use continuous reinforcement when first teaching a behavior and placing it on cue.

**Key points:**

- Always strive for stimulus control (your dog knows the cue) when training.

- Competitive trainers will want behavioral fluency in their dogs.

- Use a continuous reinforcement schedule when teaching a new behavior and until there is stimulus control.

Through the use of continuous and positive reinforcement, the cue for the behavior and the behavior itself takes on reinforcing properties. That is, if every cued sit is rewarded, the sit cue has a strong predictive value to your dog of receiving a reward. The cue will cause a positive emotional response in your dog. The power of continuous and positive reinforcement is that cued behaviors taught with this schedule can be used to reinforce other behavioral responses.

Once a behavioral response is placed on cue and learned in a variety of environmental contexts or situations, then reinforcement or rewards are switched to a partial or intermittent reinforcement schedule.

## *Partial or Intermittent Reinforcement (PRF)*

The behavioral response is reinforced only part of the time or intermittently with a partial reinforcement schedule. For example, in a training session using partial reinforcement, your dog is not offered a treat every time he sits. The frequency of treating will depend on the schedule. If the behavior is not sufficiently reinforced it will go extinct or cease to occur. Learned behaviors are acquired more slowly when initially taught using partial reinforcement. A partial reinforcement schedule should be used only after a sufficient history of continuous reinforcement. The power of partial reinforcement is that behavioral responses are more resistant to extinction. Your dog never knows when he is going to win the jackpot and in order to win he has to continue to play.

There are many different schedules for partial reinforcement: fixed ratio, variable ratio, fixed interval, or variable interval. In training your dog you will eventually use a variable ratio schedule of reinforcement. Ratio refers to the number of responses between reinforcement. With variable reinforcement schedules, the rate of reinforcement is unpredictable to your dog. For example, the ratio would be variable if your dog has to sit 5 times, 3 times, 7 times, or 1 time prior to obtaining a treat. Gambling or playing a slot machine is an example of a reward based on a variable ratio schedule. This makes for very persistent behavior. Use caution when implementing intermittent reinforcement. If the rate of reinforcement is not sufficient, your dog may decide to stop performing the behavior all together. The necessary rate of reinforcement will depend on your dog and the context. More harm than good is done by attempting to transition to an intermittent reinforcement schedule too soon.

**Key points:**

- A partial reinforcement schedule should be used only after a sufficient history of continuous reinforcement.

- If the rate of reinforcement is not sufficient, your dog may decide to stop performing the behavior all together.

- Attempting to transition to an intermittent reinforcement schedule too soon can be problematic.

## Competing Motivation

There are times in our lives and our dog's lives that competing motivations will alter our behavioral response. While at home relaxing and immersed in watching a movie, I may decide to ignore the ringing phone. Although I understand the meaning of the phone ringing and I enjoy talking on the phone, I would rather stay in my comfortable spot on the couch and watch the movie. Your dog will be faced with competing motivations all the time, including an interesting smell, other dogs, animals, or people.

When teaching new behaviors, a non-distracting environment is a necessity. Just as it would be difficult for you to master a new skill while at a football game or music concert, your dog will be more successful and attentive if you provide an appropriate learning environment. Other pets in the house should be managed away from the training area. Initial training sessions should occur in a quiet location free of interruptions. Your attention should be focused on your dog throughout the lesson. You are asking him to pay attention to you and the same courtesy should be given to him throughout the training session.

We recommend using a verbal cue to initiate a training session. This tells your dog to pay attention to you and that you are paying attention to him. You might say "ready" or "training." Similarly and more importantly, use a verbal cue to communicate to your dog the end of a training session. Tell your dog, "done," so he knows you are not ignoring him, just that the training session is over. With your "done" cue, offer your dog a longer-lasting treat or a self-entertaining toy.

**Key points:**

- Competing motivations will alter behavioral responses.
- When teaching a new behavior, always begin in a non-distracting environment.

The predatory nature of dogs may make it difficult to learn or practice a new behavior with the distraction of ducks and geese in the distance.

# Rules of Clicker Training

1. Click then treat.

2. The treat hand should remain still until after the click.

3. Even if you accidently click, follow it up with a reward.

4. The clicker is used to teach new behaviors. Once the behavior is under stimulus control, the clicker can be faded.

5. Keep sessions short (2 to 5 minutes). Several short sessions will be more productive than one long session.

6. End training sessions on a "good paw." After you have made a breakthrough, do not be tempted to go further in that training session.

7. Vary the complexity of the exercise. Avoid always making it more difficult.

8. Set your dog up to succeed. Dogs learn better the more often they get it right. If your dog is not successful, you are asking for too much, too soon. You and your dog will quickly get frustrated. Remember training should be a fun game!

9. Work on only one new behavior that is not on cue at each training session.

10. Train the dog in a quiet environment with few distractions. Once the response is learned there, move the training location to progressively more complex and stimulating environments. The dog will have to be trained in each environment that you wish him to respond. You may start in the living room of your home. Later, move on to the kitchen, backyard, front yard, park, etc.

11. Appropriate responses should be rewarded within half a second of the behavior being completed.

12. The dog will learn most rapidly if every desired response is rewarded. Once the behavior is established, reward it intermittently. This will make the response more permanent because it creates anticipation of reward. Your dog is never sure when he will hit the jackpot.

13. Once the dog has learned the behavior from one person, have other members of the family train him to respond to them. If the dog knows the cue well, this should not take long.

14. Punishment does not work in teaching behavior. The opposite of a reward is no reward, not punishment! Punishment may frighten or excite your dog, which reduces his ability to learn.

## References

1.   Wood, L. 2006. An Analysis of the Efficacy of Bridging Stimuli: Comparing the clicker to a verbal bridge. Unpublished master's thesis, Hunter College, New York.

# FOUNDATION TRAINING EXERCISES

## Foundation Behaviors

Foundation behaviors are basic behaviors we teach our dogs in order to improve our communication with them. They are the building blocks for all future training and learning, whether you hope to train your dog on a competitive level or just want your puppy to have manners. Foundation training is where you should begin.

## Getting Started

The training section is outlined utilizing markers, whether using a mechanical marker (clicker) or a verbal marker ("yes"). Training instructions refer to the use of a clicker because it is the preferable marker for teaching new behaviors. For simplicity, click and treat is abbreviated in the text as CT.

The introduction of each exercise outlines the goals, importance, training tools, and commonly used cues for each behavior. In addition, helpful hints are provided. Be prepared for each session; decide on your cue and have your training tools readily accessible. Your dog should be hungry and you both should be ready to have fun.

Training outlines are guidelines for teaching your dog new skills. Whether you are beginning foundation training with a puppy or an adult dog, all dogs have the capacity to learn these skills. Be patient and realize each dog will acquire skills at different rates.

To compensate for variation in learning, we have provided different ways of reaching the goal behavior. Methods for getting the behavior may include *Capturing*, *Targeting*, or *Luring*. For some exercises at *Level 1: Get the Behavior*, you will have to choose a method for training. You will then progress through the levels of training to include adding the verbal cue and teaching the behavior under distraction, with duration, or at a distance when applicable.

Outlines for teaching the following behaviors are included:

- Attention
- Targeting
- Recall
- Sit
- Down
- Place
- Loose leash walking
- Bring
- Drop it
- Leave it

**Key points:**

- Foundation behaviors are the building blocks for future training.
- Markers will be used to teach new behaviors.
- Click and treat will be abbreviated CT.

# ATTENTION

## Introduction

**Goal:** Dog looks to handler's eyes when cued.

**Importance:** The first step in teaching a behavior is having your dog's attention. This cue can be used for refocusing your dog's attention on you in a variety of situations. When your dog is focused on listening to you, training is more successful.

**Training Tools:** Clicker and treats.

**Cue:** "Watch," "Watch me," "Look," "Eyes."

### *Helpful Hints*

- Avoid using the dogs name as the cue because it is overused and not reinforced sufficiently outside of training.

- Do not click and reward any other offered behaviors (barking, jumping, mouthing). Reinforce quiet attention (eye contact).

- When initially training small dogs, sitting on the floor may be easier because the dog does not have to look up as far.

- When first teaching attention, if you are having trouble getting your dog to look at you, a kissing noise may be used (once or twice) to prompt your dog to look at your face.

- Delivering (spitting) treats from your mouth to your dog is helpful. Your dog will want to stare at your face.

# ATTENTION: CAPTURE METHOD

## Level 1: Get the Behavior

1. Click the instant your dog looks at your face.

2. Toss a treat on the floor. Vary where the treat is tossed. Alternate between tossing the treat on the ground and offering a treat from your hand. By tossing the treat, you reset your dog to offer the behavior again, rather than just sitting and staring at you.

3. Practice 1 to 2 times a day for 10 to 20 repetitions. Repeat until your dog is reliably looking at your face/ eyes to earn a CT.

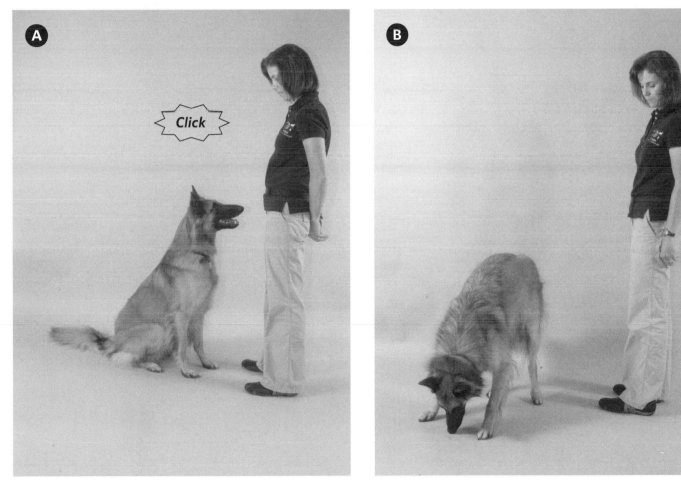

**A.** Click the instant your dog makes eye contact, regardless of his body position (sitting, standing, or lying down).

**B.** Toss a food treat on the ground to reset your dog. Wait for eye contact and repeat the steps.

# ATTENTION: CAPTURE METHOD
## Level 2: Add the Cue

4. Add the cue once the behavior is predictable. When your dog finishes eating the treat and begins to turn to look at you, give your verbal cue. The verbal cue should precede eye contact. Repeat 10 times.

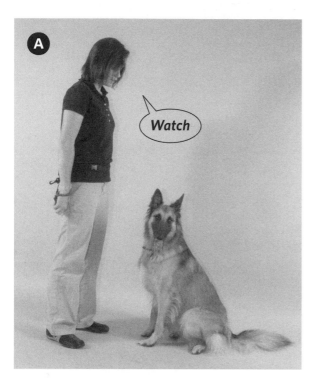

**A.** Add the cue, "Watch," just prior to eye contact.

**B.** Click the second your dog looks at your eyes.

**C.** Reward with a food treat.

# ATTENTION: CAPTURE METHOD
## Level 3: Distraction, Duration, & Distance

5. Add distraction once your dog has learned the cue in one location. Vary the location and your body position relative to your dog. Train in other areas of the house, in the backyard, front yard, in the car, on a walk, at the park, etc.

6. Add duration once you have trained attention in 10 different locations and under distraction. Return to the least distracting environment and begin to add duration. Your dog now needs to hold the eye contact for 1 second/CT, 2 seconds/CT, 3 seconds/CT. Progressively increase the duration of eye contact. Vary the duration so it does not always get more difficult. Sometimes it is a 5-second delay/CT and other times no delay/CT. Start with a 1-second duration/CT when beginning in a new environment.

7. Add distance once you have trained the behavior under distraction and with duration. Return to the least distracting environment and begin to add distance.

**A.** Add the distraction of a treat in each hand. Give the "Watch" cue.

**B.** Click the second your dog makes eye contact.

**C.** Alternate delivering the treat from your left and right hand and tossing it on the ground.

# TARGETING
## Introduction

**Goal:** Dog touches nose to an object on cue.

**Importance:** Learning to touch and follow a target allows you to teach a variety of behaviors, including come, sit, over or under an obstacle, loose leash walking, and spin, to name a few. Targeting is preferable to luring a behavior with a treat.

**Training tools:** Clicker, treats, target stick.

**Cue:** "Touch," "Spot," "Nose."

### *Helpful Hints*

• Click while your dog's nose is touching the target. A late click actually teaches him to back away from the target.

• If your dog is hesitant to approach the target, you may be presenting the target too far away from your dog's nose or he is afraid of the target. If your dog is afraid of the target, you may initially place treats on the target.

• Treat training has relied heavily on having the dog follow a treat to prompt a desired behavior (luring). Although dogs will learn the behavior, it takes longer to fade a treat than to fade a target. We want your dog to follow the target, not a treat.

• When teaching your dog to wait for the cue, make sure he is successful 80 to 90% of the time, otherwise he may give up.

# TARGETING: CAPTURE METHOD
## Level 1: Get the Behavior

1. Present the end of the target stick and hold it steady a few inches in front of your dog's nose.

2. Click and treat your dog for touching his nose to the target. The click should occur while his nose is touching the target. Remove the target as you offer your dog a treat. Repeat 5 times.

3. Present the target stick 1 to 2 inches to the *right* of your dog's nose, 1 to 2 inches to the *left* of your dog's nose, then 1 to 2 inches *below* and above your dog's nose. CT successful responses. Repeat each position 5 to 10 times.

**A.** Present the target stick in front of your dog's nose. Click the instant his nose touches the stick.

**B.** Remove the target stick as you offer a food treat.

# TARGETING: CAPTURE METHOD
## Level 2: Add the Cue

4. Once your dog is reliably touching the tip of the target stick with his nose, add the verbal cue. Right now the cue to the dog is the presentation of the stick. In order to change it from the visual cue (the target stick) to a verbal cue, "touch," do the following:

   a. Prior to presenting the stick, say "touch." Present the stick. Click the nose touch, remove the stick and offer a treat. Repeat 10 times.

   b. Say "touch," present stick, click and treat. Do not remove the target stick. As your dog is eating the treat, say "touch" and move the target stick about 6 inches away, so he has to follow it. Click and treat. Repeat 10 times You are no longer removing the target stick, simply moving the position of the stick in relation to your dog. Give the verbal cue before he starts to move for the stick.

   c. Allow your dog to touch the target stick prior to giving the verbal cue one time. Do not CT because you have not given the verbal cue. When your dog backs away, say "touch," and CT the nose touch. One out of ten times, purposely pause a second after your dog consumes the treat. If he does not immediately go to touch the target stick, give the cue, "touch" and CT. If he touches the stick prior to the verbal cue, do not CT. He is learning to wait for the cue.

**A.** Give the cue, "Touch," prior to presenting the target stick.

**B.** Click the instant your dog's nose touches the stick.

**C.** Remove the target stick as you offer a food treat.

# TARGETING: CAPTURE METHOD
## Level 3: Distraction, Duration, & Distance

5. Add distraction once your dog has learned targeting in one location. Vary the presentation of the target and your body position relative to your dog. Train in other areas of the house, in the backyard, front yard, on a walk, at the park, etc.

6. Add duration once you have trained targeting in 10 different locations and under distraction. Return to the least distracting environment and begin to add duration. Your dog now needs to hold the nose contact for 1 second/CT, 2 seconds/CT, 3 seconds/CT. Progressively increase the duration of nose contact. Vary the duration so it does not always get more difficult. Sometimes it is a 5-second pause/CT and other times no pause/CT. Start with a 1-second duration/CT when beginning in a new environment.

7. Add distance once you have trained targeting in 10 different locations, under distraction, and with duration. Return to the least distracting environment and begin to add distance. Your dog now needs to follow the target with his nose for 1 step/CT, 2 steps/CT, 3 steps/CT. Progressively increase the distance that the target is away from your dog. Vary the distance so it does not always get more difficult. Sometimes it is 5 steps of targeting/CT and other times one step/CT. Start with 1 step/CT when beginning in a new environment.

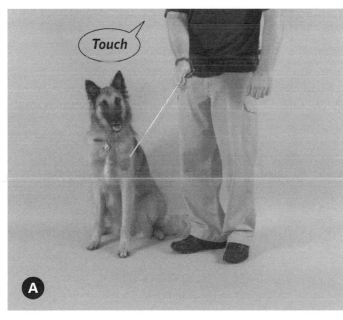

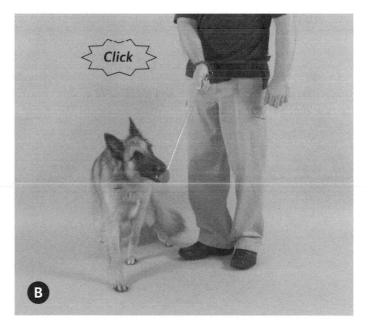

**A.** When adding distance, present the target stick a few feet in front of your dog's nose.

**B.** Click as he follows the target stick.

# TARGETING: CAPTURE METHOD
## Level 4: Generalization

8. When your dog responds to the "touch" cue 80% of the time, begin to have him target other novel objects. These objects may include nail trimmer, dog brush, ear cleaner, etc. Teach your dog to target your hand, objects in your hand, objects away from you, and objects on the ground.

**A.** Generalizing the cue, "Touch," to a novel object.

**B.** Click the instant his nose touches the target.

# RECALL

## Introduction

**Goal:** Dog runs directly to you when cued.

**Importance:** A solid recall is the most important cue you will teach your dog. This behavior can save your dog's life should he get away from you.

**Training Tools:** Clicker, treats, collar, leash.

**Cue:** "Come," "Here," "Front."

### *Helpful Hints*

- Use a long leash and collar or harness when in an unsecure public area.
- When your dog comes to you, no matter what he was doing when you called him, always *reward* him!
- Pick a new cue word if you have already been using a word to call your dog, especially if the word has been overused, under reinforced, or has a negative connotation.
- Avoid threatening body language such as staring at your dog, leaning over, or reaching for your dog when he is backing away. You are unintentionally giving him body language that tells him to not come close.
- Do not play "keep away" games in which you run after your dog. This teaches your dog it is a fun game to run from people and avoid getting caught. Only encourage your dog to chase you and come to you.
- Use the opposition reflex. Have a person hold your dog by his collar/leash as you run away from your dog. The person should release the dog after you give the recall cue.
- Play round robin between two or more people standing apart from each other. Call your dog back and forth between the people for a reward. One person should call the dog and excitedly back away, CT the behavior, and then ignore. At this point the next person should call the dog, excitedly back away, and CT the behavior. Your dog will quickly learn to come when called. Do not reward the behavior if you have not given the cue.
- Never call your dog (just go and get him) if you are going to do something that he may find undesirable (trim his nails, give him a bath, etc). Otherwise, you are poisoning your cue.

# RECALL

## Level 1: Run with Me

1. With your dog at your left or right side, give the verbal cue, "Come," and then briskly run forward to the end of your leash or 6 to 12 feet away from your dog.

2. As your dog follows you, click.

3. Slow down enough so your dog is able to catch you. Offer a treat with your left or right hand. Repeat 10 times.

**A.** With your dog at your side, give the cue, "Come," just prior to moving forward.

**B.** Click as your dog runs to catch up with you.

**C.** Slow your pace and offer a food treat from your hand.

# RECALL

## Level 2: Front

4. With your dog in front of you, give the verbal cue, "Come," and then back 6 to 12 feet away from your dog.

5. Click as your dog takes the initial step towards you.

6. Offer the treat square in front of your body between your legs. This teaches your dog to come directly in front of you. Repeat 10 times.

**A.** With your dog in front of you, give the cue, "Come," just prior to moving backward.

**B.** Click as your dog is moving towards you.

**C.** Slow your pace and offer food treats from both hands between your legs.

### The Collar Grab

Some dogs will shy away when a person reaches for their collar. There is nothing more frustrating and frightening than when your dog comes to you and you reach for him and he backs away just out of reach. Teaching the recall is an important time to get your dog accustomed to his collar being grabbed. Incorporate the collar grab into the delivery of the treat. The dog comes to you and as you reach down to give him the treat, gently reach under his chin and slip your fingers under his collar.

# RECALL
## Level 3: Distance

7. Add distance by gradually increasing how far you are from your dog when calling him. A "stay" cue or person holding your dog's leash is helpful when adding distance. Another alternative is to use a harness (to prevent damage to your dog's neck) and lunge line around a post.

**A.** Increase your distance from your dog gradually. A long lunge line is attached for safety.

**B.** Click as your dog runs toward you. Backing away from your dog encourages him to come. Reward him with a food treat or a toy when he gets to you.

# RECALL

## Level 4: Speed

8.  With your dog at a distance from you, give the verbal cue, "Come," and then back away from your dog.

9.  Click as your dog is coming toward you. Just before your dog reaches you, open your legs and toss a treat or toy between your legs. Your dog should run between your legs to retrieve the treat or toy.

10. As your dog eats the treat or fetches the toy, back away in the other direction and repeat. If using a toy you will need at least two. This method teaches your dog to run fast towards you and to not hesitate upon arrival.

**A.** Variation using a harness and lunge line around a post to hold the dog at a distance until cued. Give the cue, "Come," and drop the line.

**B.** Click as your dog reaches his maximum speed toward you and prepare to toss a toy between your legs.

**C.** Toss the toy between your legs. As your dog retrieves the toy or treat, turn and back away from your dog and repeat.

# RECALL

## Level 5: Distraction

11. Add distractions once your dog has learned the cue in one location. Vary the location and your body position relative to your dog. If your training is geared towards formal competition, you may choose to only reward your dog for coming directly in front of you. Other options would be to teach him to come to your left side and sit. Teach the recall in different areas of the house, in the backyard, front yard, on a walk, at the park, etc.

Change your body position relative to your dog when teaching a recall.

# SIT

## Introduction

**Goal:** Dog places its rear on the ground when cued.

**Importance:** The sit cue is the first stationary behavior you will teach your dog. Sit means touch your bottom to the ground and do not move. In essence, you will teach the sit as a duration behavior resulting in a sit-stay.

**Training Tools:** Clicker, target stick, treats.

**Cue:** "Sit."

### Helpful Hints

- If having difficulty reaching the goal, shape the behavior. CT small increments toward the desired behavior until your dog's rear touches the ground.

- If your dog backs away from you, move the target or treat hand towards you initially prior to rearward movement. This will prompt your puppy to move toward you slightly. In addition, teach the behavior along a wall or physical barrier to prevent backing up.

- Do not use your dog's name prior to the sit cue because it makes it difficult to learn the single word "sit." Your dog will think the cue is "Fido sit."

- When teaching duration or distance, if your dog breaks the sit, you have increased the criteria too rapidly or the environment is too distracting.

- Vary the duration or distance so it is not always more difficult with each repetition.

- When teaching duration, reward your dog with a treat while he is in the sit position.

# SIT: CAPTURE METHOD

## Level 1: Get the Behavior

1. Observe your dog and wait for him to offer a sit.

2. Click the instant your dog's bottom touches the ground.

3. Alternate between offering your dog a treat from your hand and tossing a treat on the ground. Tossing a treat on the ground resets your dog to sit again.

4. Repeat until your dog is reliably offering a sit to earn a CT.

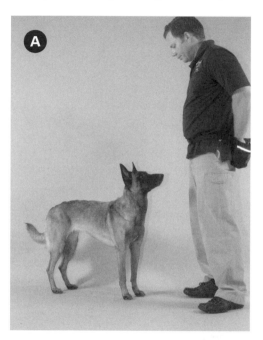
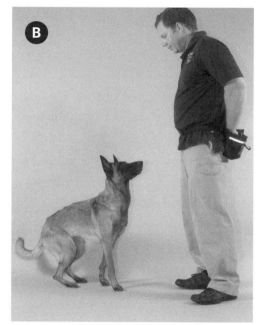

**A.** Observe your dog and wait for him to offer the sit.

**B.** Almost there.

**C.** Click the second his rear touches the ground.

**D.** Reward with a food treat.

# SIT: TARGET METHOD

## Level 1: Get the Behavior

1. Position the target stick a few inches in front of your dog's nose.

2. Slowly move the target stick upward between your dog's eyes and ears towards his rear. As your dog's head lifts up, in a gentle rocking motion his rear should approach the ground.

3. Click the instant your dog's rear touches the ground and offer a treat.

4. Repeat until your dog is reliably sitting when prompted by your target stick to earn a CT.

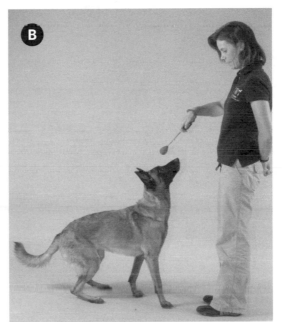

**A.** Present the target stick in front of your dog's nose.

**B.** Slowly move the target stick over his head.

Click

**C.** Click the second his rear touches the ground.

**D.** Reward with a food treat.

# SIT: LURE METHOD
## Level 1: Get the Behavior

1. Position a treat about 1 inch in front of your dog's nose.

2. Slowly move the treat upward between your dog's eyes and ears towards his rear. As your dog's head lifts up, in a gentle rocking motion his rear should approach the ground.

3. Click the instant your dog's rear touches the ground and offer a treat.

4. After a few repetitions, you should be able to lure the behavior without a treat in your hand. Repeat until your dog is reliably sitting when prompted by your hand movement to earn a CT.

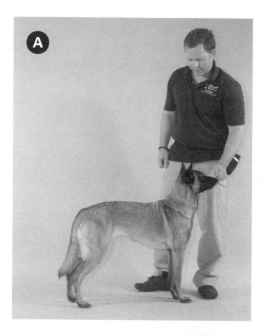

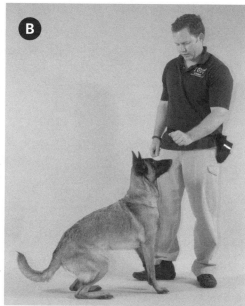

**A.** Lure your dog with a treat in your hand just in front of his nose.

**B.** Almost there.

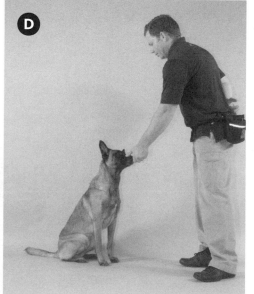

**C.** Click the second his rear touches the ground.

**D.** Reward with a food treat.

# SIT: CAPTURE, TARGET, OR LURE METHOD

## Level 2: Add the Cue

5.  Add the cue once the behavior is predictable. Just prior to your dog offering the sit, give your verbal cue. The verbal cue, "sit," should precede any hand or target movement and your dog's rear touching the ground. Repeat.

6.  Teaching the relevance of the verbal cue: Allow your dog to sit prior to giving the cue one time out of 20. Do not CT. Take a step away from him so he moves or gets up. Give your sit cue. When his bottom touches the ground, CT.

Capturing: Add the cue, "Sit," just prior to your dog offering the sit position.

Targeting: Add the cue, "Sit," just prior to moving the target stick. Almost there.

Luring: Add the cue, "Sit," just prior to moving your hand.

# SIT: CAPTURE, TARGET, OR LURE METHOD
## Level 3: Distraction, Duration, & Distance

7. Add distractions once your dog has learned the cue in one location. Vary the location; train in other areas of the house, in the backyard, front yard, on a walk, in the park, etc. Vary your body position relative to your dog; turn sideways to where your dog is at your side, wave your arms, recline in a chair, etc.

8. Add duration once you have trained sit in 10 different locations and under distraction. Return to the least distracting environment and begin to add duration. Your dog now needs to hold the sit for 1 second/CT, 2 seconds/CT, 3 seconds/CT, etc. Progressively increase the duration of the behavior. Sometimes, it is 5 seconds/CT and other times no pause/CT. Start with only a 1-second delay/CT when beginning in a new environment.

9. Add distance once you have trained duration with distractions. Here we require your dog to maintain the behavior as you take a step away from him. Begin in a non-distracting environment and reset the duration to a few seconds. The distraction is your body movement away from your dog. Cue your dog to sit. Lean away from him and CT. Toss a treat to reset him. Cue your dog to sit. Take 1 step away and return and CT. Toss a treat to reset him. Gradually, increase the distance away.

**A1**   Distraction: "Sit" cued while walking

**A2**   Distraction: "Sit" while handler continues to walk

**B1**   "Sit" at a distance

**B2**   Good boy!

# DOWN

## Introduction

**Goal:** Dog places his elbows and rear on the ground when cued.

**Importance:** The down cue is the second stationary behavior taught as a duration behavior resulting in a down-stay. Down means touch your elbows and rear to the ground.

**Training Tools:** Clicker, treats.

**Cue:** "Down."

### *Helpful Hints*

- The behavior may be taught with your dog in a sitting or standing position.

- Having difficulty getting the entire behavior? Use shaping. CT small increments toward the desired behavior until your dog's elbows and rear touch the ground. This may mean clicking and treating prior to the elbows touching the ground.

- High-energy dogs may find the down more difficult to perform because it requires greater relaxation and composure.

- If your dog backs away from you, move the target or treat toward you initially prior to rearward movement. In addition, teach the behavior along a wall or physical barrier to prevent backing up.

- Do not use your dog's name prior to the down cue because it makes it difficult to learn the single word "down."

- When teaching duration, if your dog breaks the down, you have increased the duration too rapidly or the environment is too distracting.

- When teaching duration, reward your dog with a treat while he is in the down position.

# DOWN: CAPTURE METHOD

## Level 1: Get the Behavior

1. Observe your dog and wait for him to lie down.

2. Click the instant his elbows and bottom touch the ground.

3. Deliver the treat and then take a few steps away to reset your dog. Vary the location of treat delivery.

4. Repeat until your dog is reliably offering a down to earn a CT.

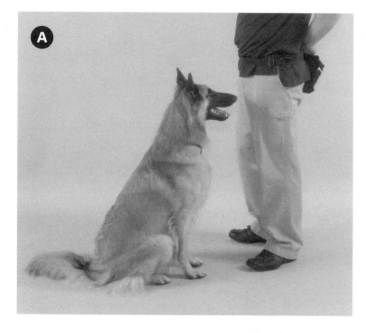

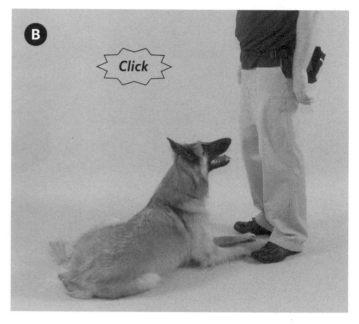

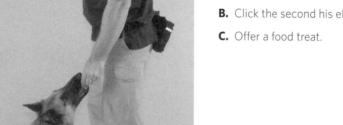

**A.** Observe your dog and wait for him to offer the down.

**B.** Click the second his elbows touch the ground.

**C.** Offer a food treat.

# DOWN: TARGET METHOD

## Level 1: Get the Behavior

1. Position the target stick about 1 inch in front of your dog's nose. Your dog may be in sitting or standing to begin this exercise.

2. Slowly move the target stick down to the ground (between your dog's paws) and back towards his elbows. As your dog's head lowers and he tucks his chin, his elbows should approach the ground.

3. Click the instant your dog's elbows and rear touch the ground and offer a treat.

4. Repeat until your dog is reliably offering a down when prompted by your target stick to earn a CT.

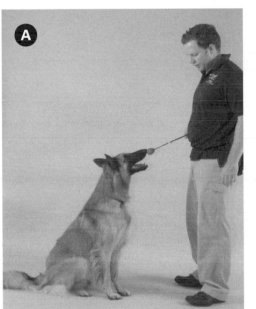

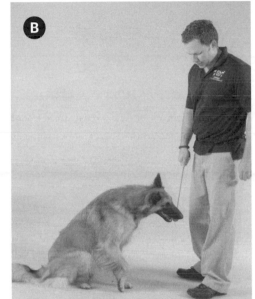

**A.** Present the target stick 1 inch in front of your dog's nose.

**B.** Lure the down by lowering the target stick to the ground.

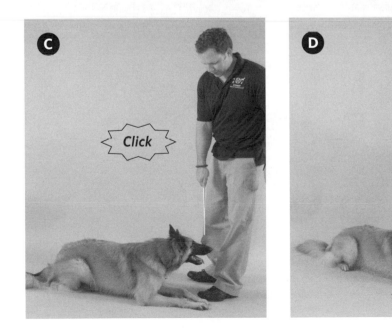

**C.** Click the second his elbows touch the ground.

**D.** Reward with a food treat.

# DOWN: LURE METHOD

## Level 1: Get the Behavior

1. Position your hand with a treat about 1 inch in front of your dog's nose.

2. Slowly move the treat hand down to the ground (between your dog's paws) and back towards his elbows. As your dog's head lowers and he tucks his chin, his elbows should approach the ground.

3. Click the instant your dog's elbows and rear touch the ground and offer a treat. Vary the location of the treat delivery. You may place the treat on the ground between his feet, toss it away from your dog, or hand it to him.

4. After a few repetitions, you should be able to lure the behavior without a treat in your hand. Repeat until your dog is reliably offering a down when prompted by a treat-free hand movement to earn a CT.

**A.** Place a treat in your hand 1 inch in front of your dog's nose.

**B.** Slowly lower your treat hand to the ground.

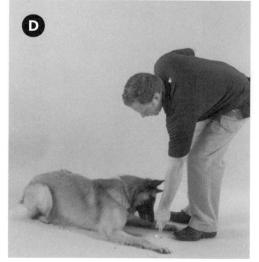

**C.** Click the second his elbows touch the ground.

**D.** Reward with a food treat between his paws.

# DOWN: CAPTURE, TARGET, OR LURE METHOD

## Level 2: Add the Cue

5. Add the cue once the behavior is predictable. Just prior to your dog lying down, give your verbal cue. The verbal cue, "down," should precede any hand or target movement. Repeat.

6. Teaching the relevance of the verbal cue: Allow your dog to offer a down prior to giving the cue one time out of 20. Do not CT. Take a step away from him so he moves or gets up. Give the "down" cue. When he goes down upon you giving the verbal cue, CT.

Capturing: Add the cue, "Down," just prior to your dog offering the down position.

Targeting: Add the cue, "Down," just prior to lowering the target stick.

Luring: Add the cue, "Down," just prior to lowering your hand.

# DOWN: CAPTURE, TARGET, OR LURE METHOD
## Level 3: Distraction, Duration, & Distance

7. Add distraction once your dog has learned the cue in one location. Vary the location; train in other areas of the house, in the backyard, front yard, on a walk, in the park, etc. Vary your body position relative to your dog; turn sideways to where your dog is at your side, wave your arms, stand on one leg, recline in a chair, etc.

8. Add duration once you have trained down in 10 different locations and under distraction. Return to the least distracting environment and begin to add duration. Your dog now needs to hold the down for 1 second/CT, 2 seconds/CT, 3 seconds/CT, etc. Progressively increase the duration of the behavior. Vary the duration so it does not always increase in difficulty. Sometimes it is 5-second down/CT and other times no pause/CT. Start with a 1-second delay/CT when beginning in a new environment.

9. Add distance once you have trained duration with distractions. Here we require your dog to maintain the behavior as you take a step away from him. Begin in a non-distracting environment and reset the duration to a few seconds. The distraction is your body movement away from your dog. Cue your dog to down. Lean away from him and CT. Toss a treat to reset him. Cue your dog to down. Take 1 step away and return and CT. Toss a treat to reset him. Gradually, increase the distance away.

Teaching fluency with the "down" cue by adding distraction, duration, and distance. Jazmin is in a down while her handler talks to a person with a dog.

# PLACE
## Introduction

**Goal:** Dog runs to a location away from you when cued.

**Importance:** This exercise teaches your dog that it can be reinforcing to go away from you. Your dog will first learn to touch his paws to a specific spot and eventually settle or stay in that specific spot. You can send your dog to this location while you are cooking, eating, or whenever you need him to be out from under foot.

**Training tools:** Clicker, treats, and a dog bed, towel, or mat.

**Cue:** "Place," "Spot," "Bed," "Mat."

### Helpful Hints
- Feeding your dog some of his meals on his place makes it a rewarding location.
- Using a slightly raised place, so that your dog has to step up to get on it, makes the location very obvious for your dog.
- Avoid talking to your dog during this exercise. Verbal encouragement can be distracting and make it more difficult for him to concentrate on the task.

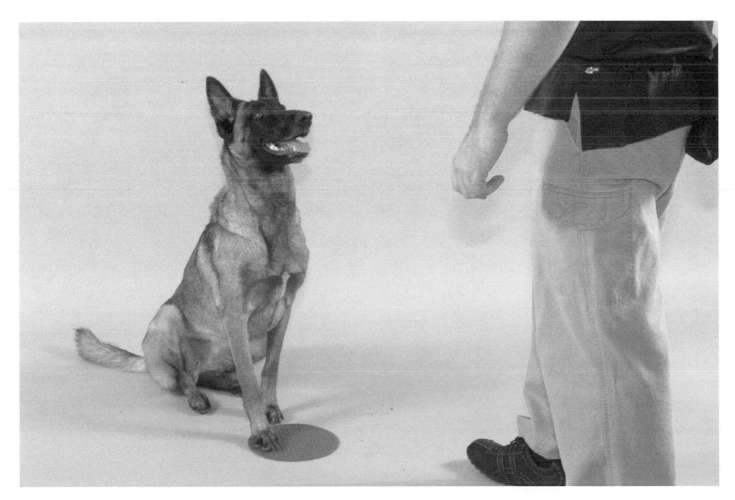

# PLACE: CAPTURE & SHAPING METHOD

## Level 1: Get the Behavior

1. Place a towel or dog bed on the floor and observe your dog until he turns his head or looks at the towel/bed.

2. Click the instant his eyes make contact with the towel/bed.

3. Toss the treat on the floor. Vary where the treat is tossed. This resets your dog to do the behavior again.

4. Gradually increase the criteria for your dog to receive a CT. Steps may include reinforcing eye contact with the bed/CT, a step towards the bed/CT, 1 foot on the bed/CT, 2 feet on the bed/CT, 4 feet on the bed/CT, offering a sit or down on the bed/CT.

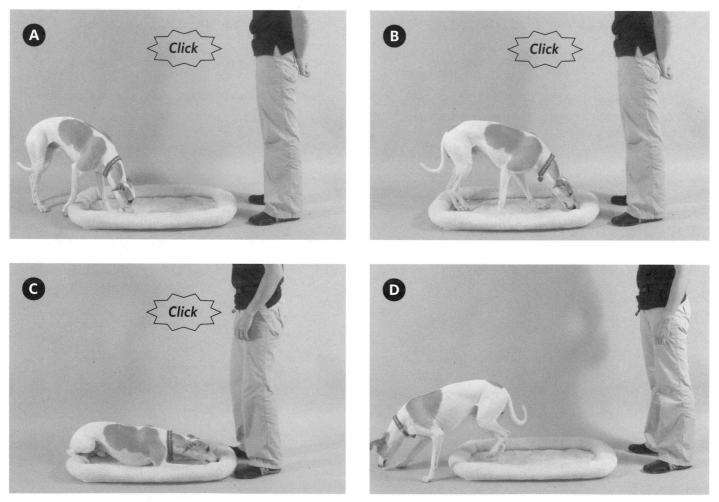

**A.** Click for one foot touching the bed, followed by tossing a treat to reset your dog (photo D).

**B.** Click for all four feet on the bed and reward with a food treat.

**C.** Click for lying down on the bed.

**D.** Toss a treat off the bed to reset your dog to perform the behavior again.

# PLACE: CAPTURE & SHAPING METHOD

## Level 2: Add the Cue

5. Add the verbal cue once the behavior is predictable. The verbal cue, "Place," should precede your dog's movement towards the bed. CT your dog for touching the place. Repeat until the behavior is reliable when cued.

**A.** Give the cue, "Place," just prior to your dog stepping on the bed.

**B.** Click when your dog has all four feet on the bed.

**C.** Alternate between offering your dog a treat on the bed and tossing a treat away from the bed.

# PLACE: LURE METHOD

## Level 1: Get the Behavior

1.  With a treat in your hand, lure your dog to his place.

2.  Motion slowly toward the place with your treat hand.

3.  Click the instant your dog's paw touches the place and offer a treat.

4.  After a few repetitions, you should be able to lure the behavior without a treat in your hand.

5.  Repeat until your dog will reliably touch the place when prompted by your hand movement or without a prompt to earn a CT.

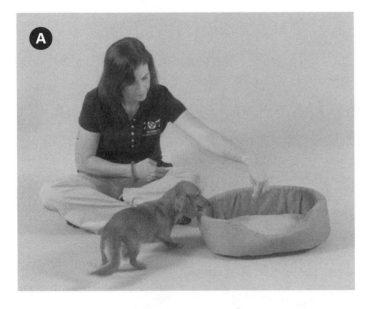

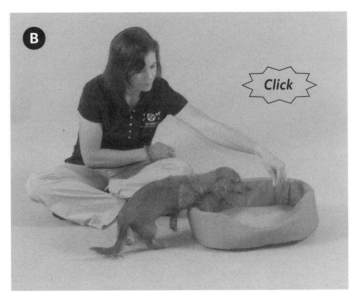

**A.** Lure your dog onto his bed with a treat in your hand.

**B.** Click the instant your dog's foot makes contact with the bed.

**C.** Reward your dog with a food treat.

# PLACE: LURE METHOD
## Level 2: Add the Cue and Fade the Lure

6. To add the verbal cue, give your cue, "Place," just a split second prior to prompting with your hand movement. Click when he is on the bed and offer a treat.

7. Begin to fade the hand movement. Give your verbal cue, "Place," and prompt with three-quarters of your hand lure. Progressively decrease to no hand signal, just a verbal cue.

8. To teach the relevance of the verbal cue, allow your dog to go to place prior to giving the cue one time out of 20. Do not CT. Take a step away from him so he moves or gets up. Give the verbal cue, "Place." When he touches the place, CT.

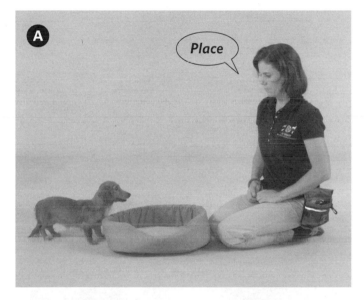

**A.** Give the cue, "Place," just prior to any hand movement.

**B.** A faded hand motion toward the bed. Click the instant your dog makes contact.

**C.** Rewarding by tossing a food treat away from the bed. Alternate your treat delivery location.

# PLACE: CAPTURE OR LURE METHOD
## Level 3: Distraction, Distance, & Duration

1.  Add distraction and distance once your dog has learned the cue in one location. Vary the location and type of place. Vary your body position and distance relative to the place.

2.  Add duration once you have trained place in 10 different locations and under distraction. Return to the least distracting environment and begin to add duration. Your dog now needs to hold the place for 1 second/CT, 2 seconds/CT, 3 seconds/CT, etc. Progressively increase the duration of the behavior. Vary the duration so it does not always increase in difficulty. Sometimes your dog will hold the position for 5 seconds/CT and other times he will be rewarded immediately. Start with a 1-second duration/CT when beginning in a new environment.

**A.** Practicing "Place" on a novel object (tree stump) and in a different environment (park).

**B.** Iliana going to "Place" after being given the verbal cue.

**C.** Iliana being clicked for sitting on "Place."

**D.** The treat is delivered to her on the place. A game of tug off the place may also be used as reinforcement for Iliana.

# LOOSE LEASH WALKING

## Introduction

**Goal:** Dog walks on leash on your left side without pulling. (This is not designed to teach a formal obedience heel for competition.)

**Importance:** Teaching your dog to walk on a loose leash will make taking him out in public more enjoyable. *Walking your dog twice a day off your property is one of the most beneficial things you can do for your dog's behavioral well-being.*

**Training tools:** Clicker, treats, leash, collar.

**Cue:** "Heel," "Let's go," "Walk," "With me," "Close."

**Preparation:** Your dog should be used to wearing a leash and collar. For simplicity, we will teach your dog to walk on your left side. To accomplish this, your treats should be delivered from your left hand, the clicker should be held in your right hand, and the leash should be tethered around your waist or held in your right hand.

### *Helpful Hints*

- Be proactive and always reward appropriate walking.

- When training small dogs, use capturing or a target stick to prevent having to walk bent over.

- Tie the leash around your waist to allow your hands to be free to deliver treats and to hold the clicker and target stick.

- Using a visual marker, such as a series of cones every few feet, reminds you to click and stop to deliver the treat. You may also use naturally occurring markers, such as lines in the sidewalk.

- Try to click when your dog looks at you to reinforce attention with walking.

- If your dog pulls ahead, stop. Do not reward pulling with forward movement. Stop and stand still. Wait until your dog's attention returns to you and then change direction.

- Ask your dog to sit when you stop and stop often. Anticipation of sitting prevents forging.

- Consider using a front clasping harness or head halter when working in an environment that is too distracting for your dog.

- Take breaks to allow your dog to explore and sniff. Consider using a cue, "Free," to signal exploration time.

Preparing to take Iris for a loose leash walk.

Notice the waist leash and treat bag. Clicker is in the right hand and treats will be delivered in the left hand.

# LOOSE LEASH WALKING: CAPTURE METHOD

## Level 1: Get the Behavior

1. Step off with your left foot. Take 1 to 2 steps. Click while you are stepping forward.

2. Stop and deliver the treat from your left hand at your side.

3. While your dog is still eating the treat, step off with your left foot. Take 1 to 2 steps and click. Stop and deliver the treat from your left hand at your side. Repeat. CT your dog for following you. With a high rate of reinforcement, your dog will anticipate treat delivery at your left side and begin walking with you.

Note: Cones are being used to illustrate the frequency of reinforcement. As the behavior becomes more reliable, the distance between the cones can be varied. A visual marker to remind the trainer to reinforce can be extremely beneficial with early training.

**A.** With your hands at your side, step off with your left foot. Click as your dog follows you.

**B.** Stop walking to deliver the treat.

**C.** As your dog finishes eating the treat, step off again on your left foot. Take 1 to 2 steps. Click as your dog follows.

**D.** Stop to deliver the treat.

**E.** Delivering the treat from your left hand at your side.

# LOOSE LEASH WALKING: CAPTURE METHOD

## Level 2: Add the Cue

4. When your dog is anticipating his position at your left side, add your verbal cue. Before taking a step, give the verbal cue, "Let's go." Take 1 to 2 steps.

5. Click as your dog is moving along side you. Stop and offer the treat from the left hand. Repeat 20 times.

**A.** Before moving forward, give the cue, "Let's go."

**B.** Step off with your left foot. Take 1 to 2 steps. Click while your dog is moving along side you.

**C.** Stop and deliver a treat from you left hand. As your dog finishes eating the treat, give the cue, "Let's go," just prior to moving forward.

# LOOSE LEASH WALKING: CAPTURE METHOD
## Level 3: Distraction & Duration

6. Add distraction by progressing to more distracting environments. Initially, start loose leash walking indoors and then progress to your backyard, front yard, walking in your neighborhood, and at a public park. Keep sessions short (3 to 5 minutes). Continue to use a high rate of reinforcement (CT every 1 to 2 steps).

7. Add duration after training in 10 different environments. Return to the least distracting environment. Gradually increase the duration between reinforcement. CT after 3 steps, 5 steps, 7 steps. Vary the duration. CT 1 step, then 5 steps, then 3 steps. Continue to stop to deliver the treat. Give the verbal cue prior to resuming forward movement.

Adding duration to loose leash walking.

**A.** After cueing, "Let's go," take 3 to 5 steps.

**B.** Click as your dog follows along side.

**C.** Stop and deliver the treat.

Note: The cones have been spread out to varying distances. Loose leash walking is a duration behavior and will take time to develop.

# LOOSE LEASH WALKING: TARGET METHOD

## Level 1: Get the Behavior

1. Step off on your left foot with your target stick in your left hand. The tip of the target stick should be a few inches in front of your dog's nose. Take 1 to 2 steps and click while your dog is following the target stick.

2. Stop and deliver the treat from your right hand. Repeat 5 times.

3. While your dog is still eating the treat, step off with your left foot. Take 1 to 2 steps and click while your dog is following the target stick but before his nose touches it. Stop and deliver the treat from your right hand. Repeat 10 to 15 times. CT your dog for following the target stick.

**A.** Step off with your left foot. The target stick should be a few inches in front of your dog's nose.

**B.** Click while your dog is following the target stick. If your dog is jumping at the stick, you may be holding it too high.

**C.** Stop to deliver the treat. Note: the target stick is pulled back and the dog is being given the treat at the handler's left side.

# LOOSE LEASH WALKING: TARGET METHOD
## Level 2: Add the Cue and Fade the Target

4. When your dog is anticipating his position at your left side, add your verbal cue. Before taking a step or presenting the target stick, give the verbal cue, "Let's go." Take 1 to 2 steps. Click as your dog is following the target stick along side you. Stop and offer the treat. Repeat 10 to 15 times.

5. Fade the target stick. Continue to repeat step 4 as you gradually shorten the length of the target stick. Eventually, your dog will be following your empty hand.

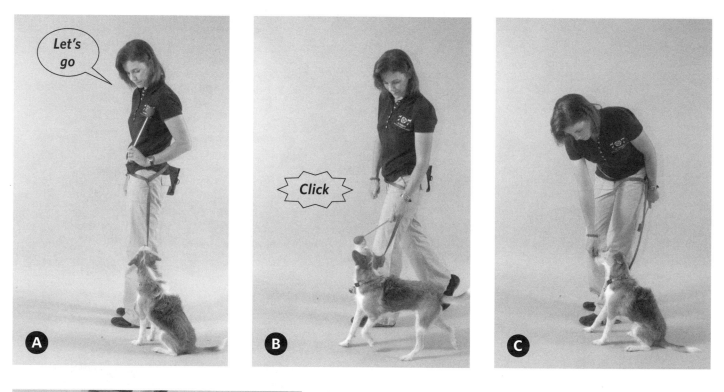

**A.** Give the cue, "Let's go," just before presenting the target stick and taking a step forward.

**B.** Take 1 to 2 steps. Click as your dog is following the target.

**C.** Stop to deliver the treat.

**D.** Fade the target stick by making it shorter.

# LOOSE LEASH WALKING: TARGET METHOD
## Level 3: Distraction & Duration

6. Add distraction by progressing to more distracting environments. You will need to repeat the previous steps in each new environment. Initially, start loose leash walking indoors and then progress to your backyard, front yard, walking in your neighborhood, and at a public park. Keep sessions short (3 to 5 minutes). Continue to use a high rate of reinforcement (CT every 1 to 2 steps).

7. Add duration after training in 10 different environments and fading the target stick. Return to the least distracting environment. Gradually increase the duration between reinforcement. CT after 3 steps, 5 steps, 7 steps. Vary the duration. CT 1 step, then 5 steps, then 3 steps. Continue to stop to deliver the treat. Give the verbal cue prior to resuming forward movement.

Iris learning loose leash walking in a new environment. A high rate of reinforcement (CT every 1 to 2 steps) is necessary in new environments. The target stick will need to be faded prior to adding duration in this environment.

# LOOSE LEASH WALKING: LURE METHOD

## Level 1: Get the Behavior

1. Holding a treat in your left hand about 1 inch in front of your dog's nose, step off on your left foot. Take 1 to 2 steps and click.

2. Stop and deliver the treat from your left hand at your side.

3. While your dog is still eating the treat, step off with your left foot and with a treat in your left hand positioned down at your side. Take 1 to 2 steps and click. Stop and deliver the treat from your left hand at your side. Repeat 10 to 15 times. CT your dog for following you. With a high rate of reinforcement, your dog will anticipate treat delivery at your left side and begin following you.

4. Holding a treat in your left hand about 1 inch in front of your dog's nose, step off on your left foot. Take 1 step and move your treat hand up to your waist and click. Deliver the treat from your left hand at your side. Repeat 10 to 15 times.

5. Holding a treat in your left hand at waist level, step off on your left foot. Take 1 to 2 steps and click. Stop and deliver the treat from your left hand at your side.

**A.** With a treat in your left hand, position your dog at your left side.

**B.** Step off on your left foot, take 1 to 2 steps. Click as your dog follows.

**C.** Stop and deliver the treat from the left hand.

**D. & E.** The next step is to move your left hand to waist level for one step. Click while your hand is up. Stop and deliver the treat.

# LOOSE LEASH WALKING: LURE METHOD
## Level 2: Add the Cue

6. When your dog is anticipating his position at your left side, add your verbal cue. Before taking a step, give the verbal cue, "Let's go." Take 1 to 2 steps.

7. Click as your dog is moving along side of you. Stop and offer the treat from the left hand. Repeat 10 to 15 times

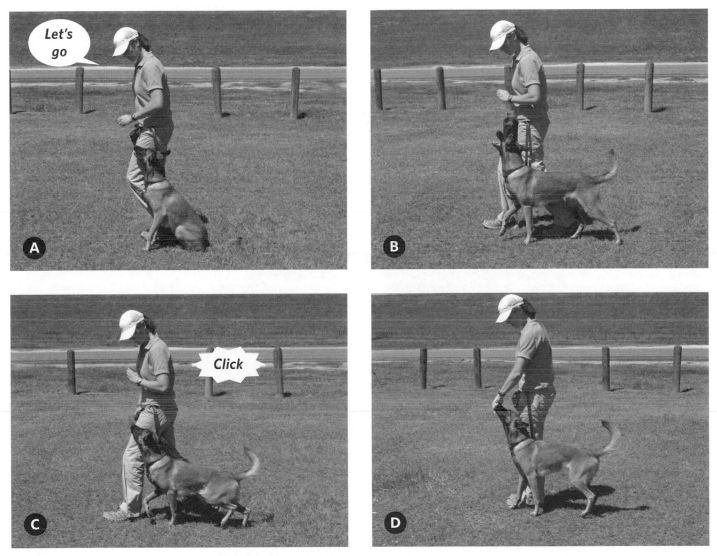

**A.** With your dog at your left side, just before taking a step give the cue, "Let's go."

**B.** Step off on your left foot, take 1 to 2 steps.

**C.** Click as your dog follows.

**D.** Stop and deliver the treat from the left hand. Before resuming loose leash walking, give the cue, "Let's go."

# LOOSE LEASH WALKING: LURE METHOD
## Level 3: Distraction & Duration

8. Add distraction by progressing to more distracting environments. You will need to repeat the previous steps in each new environment. Initially, start loose leash walking indoors and then progress to your backyard, front yard, walking in your neighborhood, and at a public park. Keep sessions short (3 to 5 minutes). Continue to use a high rate of reinforcement (CT every 1 to 2 steps).

9. Add duration after training in 10 different environments and fading the food lure. Return to the least distracting environment. Gradually increase the duration between reinforcement. CT after 3 steps, 5 steps, 7 steps. Vary the duration. CT 1 step, then 5 steps, then 3 steps. Continue to stop to deliver the treat. Give the verbal cue prior to resuming forward movement.

In novel and distracting environments, a high rate of reinforcement will be necessary at first. Keep sessions short and fun.

# BRING

## Introduction

**Goal:** Dog picks up a toy/object and returns it to you.

**Importance:** A retrieve is a valuable way to exercise your dog and engage him in appropriate play. You want your dog to bring toys and objects to you, instead of running away with them.

**Training tools:** Clicker, treats, leash and collar, a favorite toy your dog will pick up in his mouth.

**Cue:** "Bring," "Get it," "Fetch."

**Preparation:** You will teach the behavior in steps utilizing a technique called "back chaining." Back chaining refers to teaching the last behavior in a sequence first. First, teach your dog to deliver the toy to your hand, while gradually increasing distance by backing away. Second, toss a toy a short distance away and have your dog bring it to you. Initially, have your dog on leash when performing the exercise. This will prevent him from running off with the toy. A leash will not be necessary (as long as you are in a secure area) once he learns how rewarding it is to bring the toy to you.

### Helpful Hints

- Teach your dog to relinquish the object on cue and incorporate "Drop it" into the exercise.
- Incorporate a sit into the exercise prior to tossing the toy and upon returning to you.
- Once your dog will drop an object on cue, engage him in a short game of tug when he returns the toy to you.
- Avoid chasing your dog when he has an object because this teaches him to run away from you.
- Let your dog bring the toy to your hands without you reaching out for the toy.
- A rope attached to the retrieve object allows you to engage your dog in tug of war at a distance.
- Only practice "Bring" for 3 to 5 minutes. It can be tiring.
- Some dogs find running after the toy more rewarding than playing tug. Use two identical toys. As your dog approaches and releases the toy, reward him by tossing the other toy in the opposite direction.
- Stand upright and take a few steps backwards as your dog approaches to encourage him to come to you.
- Clapping your hands while backing away encourages your dog to come and play with you.
- Avoid discouraging your young dog from picking objects up in his mouth if you want to teach your dog to retrieve. If he has an inappropriate object, use your "Drop it" cue and reward relinquishment, or, if your dog has not learned "Drop it," do an exchange for a treat.

# BRING: CAPTURE METHOD

## Level 1: Get the Behavior

1. With your dog on leash in front of you, offer your dog a toy he is likely to take in his mouth.

2. Once he takes the toy, back one step away. Hold your hand down close to your body.

3. As he follows, click. Click before he drops the toy. Stop backing up and offer a treat. You may need to present the treat directly in front of his nose. The treat should prompt him to drop the toy.

4. Repeat steps 1 to 3, five times.

5. Repeat steps 1 to 2, but wait to click until your dog touches the toy to your hand. Offer a treat. If your dog knows hand targeting, you can cue him to target your hand while he holds the toy and approaches you.

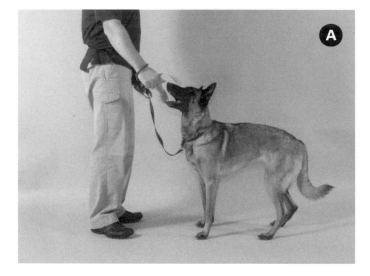

**A.** Offer your dog a toy he is likely to take in his mouth.

**B1.** With the toy in his mouth, take a step backward such that your dog has to follow. You may prompt your dog to follow you by patting your legs or using gentle leash tension. Click him for following with the toy in his mouth. Reward with a food treat.

**B2.** Click for touching the toy to your hand. Reward with a food treat. Clicking or offering the treat will likely prompt releasing the object.

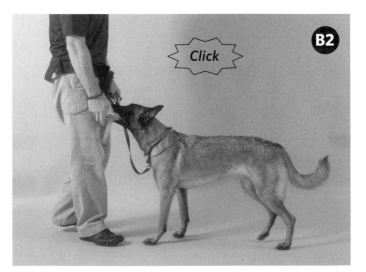

# BRING: CAPTURE METHOD

## Level 2: Add the Cue

6. Add the verbal cue once your dog is reliably touching the toy to your hand. Give your dog the toy. With the toy in his mouth, say your verbal cue and take a step back. When the toy touches your hand, CT.

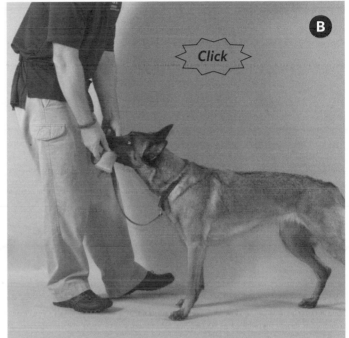

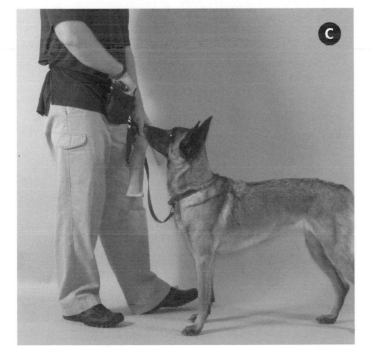

**A.** With the toy in your dog's mouth, give the cue, "Bring."

**B.** Take a step backward such that your dog has to follow. Click for touching the toy to your hand.

**C.** Reward with a food treat from your hand.

# BRING: CAPTURE METHOD

## Level 3: Duration

7. With the toy in your dog's mouth, add duration by moving several steps back away from your dog so that he has to carry the toy further to get to you.

8. CT touching the toy to your hand.

**A.** After your dog has taken the toy in his mouth, step backwards.

**B.** Backing away from your dog will encourage him to follow you.

**C.** Click when your dog brings the toy to your hand, and give him a treat..

# BRING: CAPTURE METHOD
## Level 4: Ground Work

9.  Place or drop the toy on the ground between you and your dog. Give your cue, "Bring," and then back 1 to 2 steps away from your dog. CT for your dog presenting the toy into your hands. (Exercise shown below)

10. Once your dog is reliably picking the toy up off the ground in front of him and bringing it to you, give your cue, "Bring," and then toss the toy on the ground at a greater distance. Initially you will give the cue prior to tossing the toy to help your dog be successful. The tossing of the toy will naturally cause him to want to chase after it. Increase the distance the toy is thrown gradually. He should pick up the toy and bring it to you. Click when he touches your hand with the toy. Offer a treat. Repeat. Alternatively, play tug when he touches the toy to your hand. (Exercise not shown)

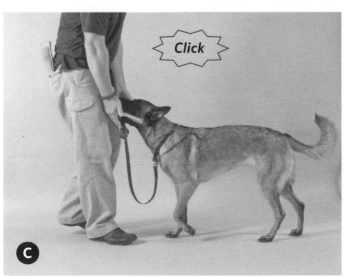

A. Place or drop the toy on the ground between you and your dog. Give the cue, "Bring."

B. Position your hands low and begin to step back as your dog picks up the toy.

C. Click when your dog brings the toy to your hand, and give him a treat.

# BRING: CAPTURE METHOD

## Level 5: Distance

11. Once your dog is proficient with Level 3 and 4, toss the toy farther.

12. Cue your dog to sit or down. Toss the toy and then give the verbal cue, "Bring." The cue will release your dog from his stationary position.

13. CT touching the toy to your hand. Repeat

**A.** Toss the toy to a greater distance. Cue your dog, "Bring."

**B.** Excitedly backing away from your dog will encourage him to bring the toy to you.

**C.** Click when your dog brings the toy to your hand, and give him a treat. Alternately, you may engage your dog in a game of tug.

# DROP IT
## Introduction

**Goal:** Dog releases an object from his mouth when cued.

**Importance:** Dogs explore the world with their mouths. At some point, your dog will have something in his mouth that you will need to get from him. If you chase your dog to grab an object from him, you will only teach him to 1) run like mad away from you, or 2) guard objects because you try to "steal" them from him. Teaching your dog to eagerly relinquish objects to you will prevent potential problems. Teaching your dog to drop it will also make it possible to play with him appropriately.

**Training tools:** Clicker, treats, objects of low value that your dog will pick up.

**Cues:** "Drop," "Out," "Give," "Drop it."

### Helpful hints

- Do not use this method when there is a history of aggression or guarding objects.
- Occasionally, offer the object (toy) back to your dog as a reward for relinquishment.
- Use a non-threatening tone of voice.

# DROP IT: CAPTURE METHOD
## Level 1: Get the Behavior

1. Offer your dog a toy he is likely to take in his mouth.

2. Observe your dog and wait until he drops the object.

3. Click as he releases the toy and offer a treat.

4. Toss or play with the toy to foster your dog's interest in picking it up again.

5. Repeat steps 2 and 3.

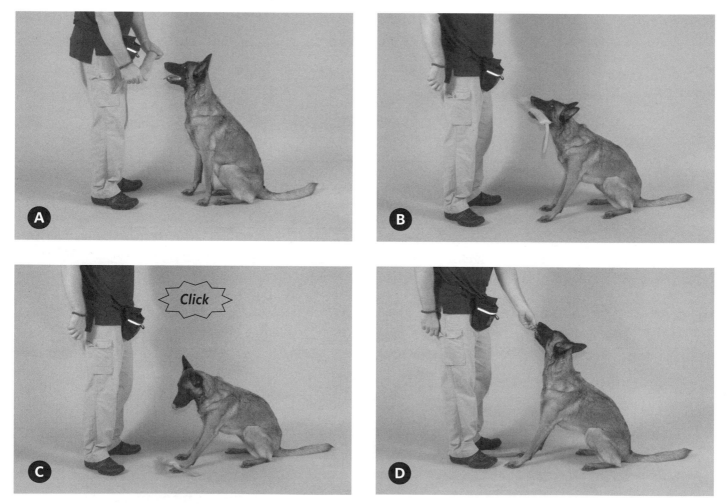

**A.** Offer your dog a toy he is likely to take in his mouth.

**B.** Wait for him to release the toy.

**C.** Click for releasing the toy from his mouth

**D.** Reward with a food treat for releasing the toy.

# DROP IT: CAPTURE METHOD
## Level 2: Add the Cue

6. Add the verbal cue, "Drop," once the behavior is predictable. The verbal cue should precede your dog releasing the toy. Repeat until the behavior is reliable when cued.

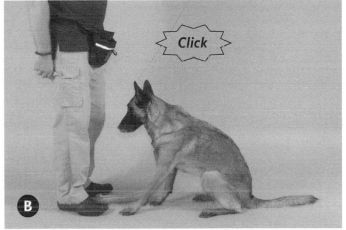

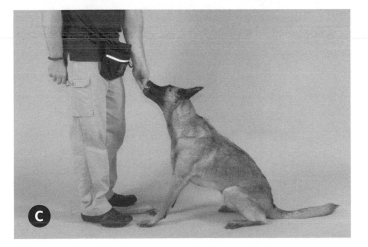

**A.** Give the cue, "Drop," just prior to your dog releasing the toy.

**B.** Click for releasing the toy.

**C.** Reward with a food treat.

# DROP IT: LURE METHOD

## Level 1: Get the Behavior

1. Offer your dog a toy he is likely to pick up in his mouth.

2. Offer your dog a food treat in front of his nose and wait until he drops the object.

3. Click as he releases the toy and give the treat.

4. Toss or play with the toy to foster interest so that your dog will pick it up again.

5. Repeat 5 times.

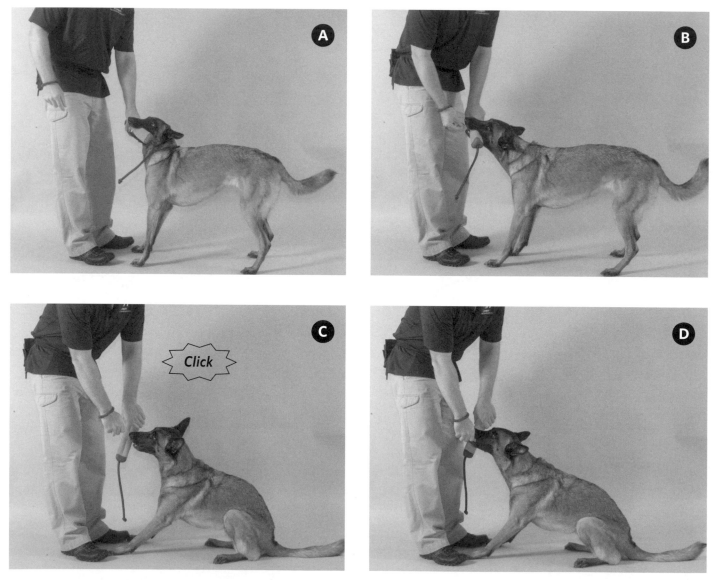

**A.** Offer your dog a toy he will take in his mouth.

**B.** Prompt your dog to release the toy with a food treat directly under his nose.

**C.** Click as your dog releases the toy.

**D.** Give a food treat.

# DROP IT: LURE METHOD

## Level 2: Add the Cue

6. Add the verbal cue, "Drop," once the behavior is able to be prompted. The verbal cue should precede offering the food treat. CT your dog for releasing the toy. Repeat this step up to 10 times.

7. Give the verbal cue, "Drop," and pause until the dog releases the toy. Click and offer your dog a treat.

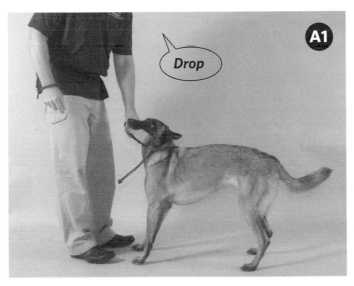

**A1.** Give the cue, "Drop," prior to moving your treat hand.

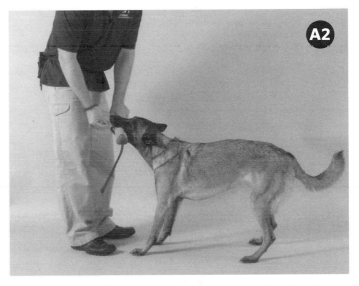

**A2.** Prompt your dog to drop the toy with a treat. When he releases, CT. Repeat 10 times.

**B1.** After completing exercise 1A & 1B, give the cue, "Drop," and wait.

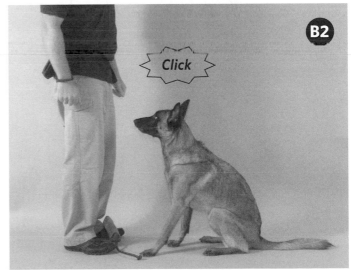

**B2.** Ideally, your dog will release the toy without the prompt of a food treat. CT. If after a few seconds he does not release, then prompt the release with a treat and repeat exercise 1A &1B.

# DROP IT: CAPTURE OR LURE METHOD
## Level 3: Distraction

8. Gradually, increase the value of the object (toy) and start over with level 1.

Offer your dog a variety of different objects and cue your dog to drop them.

The more novel and exciting the object, the more valuable it is to your dog.

Your dog will have individual preferences.

Generally, soft and plush objects are preferable to rubber or hard ones.

When teaching drop with a new object, expect to begin at level 1.

# LEAVE IT
## Introduction

**Goal:** Dog ignores object and looks to handler when cued.

**Importance:** "Leave it" allows you to communicate to your dog not to pick up objects in his mouth. Similar to the cue, "Drop it," "Leave it" refers to preventing your dog from picking up an object. When teaching the cue, "leave it," the reward should come from you and should not be the object your dog was asked to leave.

**Training tools:** Clicker, treats, a treat/object of low value.

**Cues:** "Leave it," "Mine," "Off."

### Helpful Hints

- Combine loose leash walking and leave it. Place toys or objects on the floor. As you approach the object, cue your dog to "Leave it," and CT from your hand. Food in closed Tupperware containers can be used as a distraction.

- Real life leave-it situations should be highly rewarded.

- Your dog needs to be successful and relaxed at each step before progressing. You do not want it to become a game of "Who can get to the treat/object faster!"

- Always use an upbeat tone of voice when cueing your dog to "Leave it."

- After your dog has learned the basics, add the attention cue or wait for eye contact before clicking.

# LEAVE IT: CAPTURE METHOD

## Level 1: Get the Behavior

1. Present a piece of food (your dog's regular food may be used) to get you dog's attention. Hold the food in your right hand. Show him the treat in an open hand.

2. When he tries to take the treat, close your hand and wait. Do not say anything or move your hand away. Your dog will attempt to take the treat out of your hand. Hold still and ignore him.

3. Wait for him to back away or move his mouth away from your hand.

4. The second your dog backs off (even if it is just a split second), click. Offer a treat from your left hand. You do not want to ever give your dog the treat/object you are asking him to leave. Repeat until the behavior is predictable; your dog is no longer trying to take the treat out of your presented hand.

5. Switch hands. "Leave it" item in left hand and the reward is presented in right hand. Repeat steps 1 to 4.

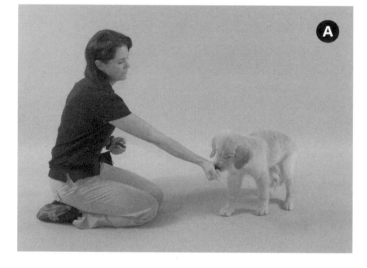

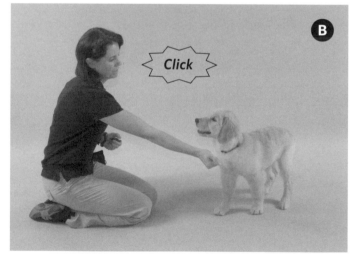

**A.** Present your dog a treat in your right hand and allow him to investigate. Hold your hand still.

**B.** Click the instant he backs away from your treat hand.

**C.** Reward with a treat from the left hand. Do not give your dog the treat in the hand from which he just backed away.

# LEAVE IT: CAPTURE METHOD
## Level 2: Add the Cue

6. Once your dog is not approaching your closed hand when presented, add the verbal cue, "Leave it," prior to presentation of your hand. CT for ignoring the presented hand. Repeat until you are able to say, "Leave it," and present the treat in your open hand without your dog attempting to take the treat.

**A.** Give the cue, "Leave it," prior to presenting your hand with a treat in it.

**B.** Click when your dog does not go for the hand. Jazmin is interested but does not attempt to take the treat from the open hand.

Note: Ideally your dog will not sniff or go towards the presented hand. Click prior to his movement. Delaying the click until your dog investigates and then backs away from the hand, teaches him to sniff the hand and then back up. You do not want your dog to chain this unwanted behavior.

**C.** Give a food treat from your other hand.

# LEAVE IT: CAPTURE METHOD
## Level 3: Generalization

7. Sit on the ground *in front* of your dog. Have your dog lie down or sit. Give your "Leave it" cue and present the treat in your open hand to your side and close to the floor. CT your dog for not moving toward the treat.

8. Gradually present the open treat hand closer to the floor until you are able to place the treat on the floor at your side and your dog will readily leave it.

9. Cue "Leave it" and drop the treat from your hand about one inch off the floor at your side. CT your dog for not moving toward the treat. Repeat while slightly increasing the distance the treat is dropped until you are standing upright. Remember to give the cue prior to dropping the treat at your side.

10. Return to sitting in front of your dog and gradually move the object closer to directly in front of your dog. Decrease the distance the treat is being dropped since we have decreased the proximity of the treat to the dog.

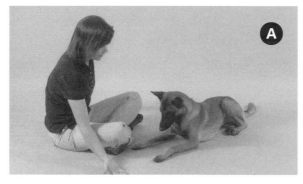

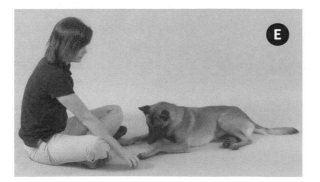

**A.** Cue "Leave it," then present the open hand with a treat to the side near the ground. CT (not shown).

**B.** Cue "Leave it," then place the treat on the ground away from the dog. CT (not shown).

**C.** Cue "Leave it," then drop the treat on the ground at a distance from the dog. CT (not shown).

**D.** Gradually drop the treat closer to the dog.

**E.** Cue "Leave it," then place the treat on the ground close to the dog. CT (not shown). This is an example of decreasing one variable (dropping), while increasing another variable (closeness).

# LEAVE IT: CAPTURE METHOD
## Level 4: Advanced Generalization

11. Generalize "Leave it" to other contexts. Place novel objects on the ground such as food or toys. While walking your dog on leash, give the cue, "Leave it," and reward with treats from your hand. To make your dog successful, start with low-value objects and progress to high-value ones. Cue your dog as you approach the object.

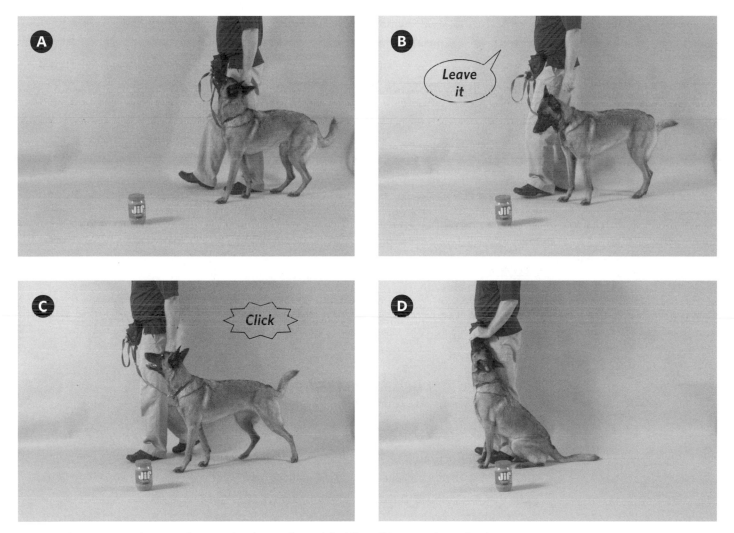

**A.** Add a distraction on the ground to practice the cue "Leave it" while walking your dog on leash.

**B.** Give the cue, "Leave it," in an upbeat tone prior to your dog investigating the object.

**C.** Click for non-interest in the object and looking to you, then continue walking a few steps.

**D.** Stop and reward with a food treat.

# APPENDIX

## Qualified Animal Behavior Professionals

Concerned about your dog's behavior? Seek guidance from a trained professional who can help determine if his behavior is abnormal with an underlying medical or behavioral component, comprising of fear, anxiety, or aggression, and prescribe appropriate treatment. Verify the qualifications of people who use titles that indicate they are animal behavior professionals. Unfortunately, the title "animal behaviorist" can be used by anyone, even a person with no formal education or training in animal behavior. Qualified animal behavior professionals include a diplomate of the American College of Veterinary Behaviorists (DACVB), a veterinarian with special interest and training in animal behavior, or a certified applied animal behaviorist (CAAB).

### *Veterinary Behaviorist*

www.veterinarybehaviorists.org

The American College of Veterinary Behaviorists is a professional organization of veterinarians who are board certified in the specialty of veterinary behavior. This veterinary specialty is recognized by the American Board of Veterinary Specialization and board-certified specialists are known as diplomates.

### *Veterinarian*

www.avsabonline.org

The American Veterinary Society of Animal Behavior (AVSAB) is a group of veterinarians and research professionals who share a special interest in the behavior of animals.

### *Certified Applied Animal Behaviorist*

www.certifiedanimalbehaviorist.com

The Animal Behavior Society (ABS) is a professional organization in North America for the study of animal behavior. Certified members come from different educational backgrounds and may include a Ph.D. in animal behavior, or doctor of veterinary medicine. Certified applied animal behaviorists, who are not veterinarians, usually work in conjunction with veterinarians to provide behavioral care.

# Professional Dog Trainers

Dog training is essentially an unlicensed and unregulated profession in the United States. Anybody who wishes to call himself or herself a dog trainer may do so without any formal education or certification. Professional trainers we recommend may include a Karen Pryor Academy Certified Training Partner, a certified professional dog trainer, or a veterinary behavior technician. However, we advise you to interview prospective trainers about their training methodology and styles to make sure they will meet your individual needs. Methodology should focus on the use of rewards (e.g., food, toys, play, affection) rather than teaching the dog using fear, pain, force, or punishment. Avoid trainers who offer guarantees. It is unethical to guarantee behavior in dogs or people.

## *Karen Pryor Academy Certified Training Partners*
www.karenpryoracademy.com

Graduates of Karen Pryor Academy are part of a community of trainers who have achieved and demonstrated a consistent level of excellence and represent themselves as a Karen Pryor Academy Certified Training Partner (KPA CTP). Training partners must teach and train using force-free principles and techniques, are subject to a policed credentialing process, and are expected to demonstrate the highest level of professionalism and ethics.

## *Certified Professional Dog Trainers*
www.ccpdt.org

The Certification Council for Professional Dog Trainers (CCPDT) is a national certification program for professional dog trainers. All certified trainers must complete a written testing, earn continuing education credits, and adhere to a code of ethics.

## *Academy of Veterinary Behavior Technicians*
www.avbt.net

A veterinary technician, after completing all requirements and testing, may become a veterinary technician specialist (VTS) in the field of behavior. VTS (Behavior) is recognized by the National Association of Veterinary Technicians in America (NAVTA) through the Academy of Veterinary Behavior Technicians. The veterinary technician who has become certified as a VTS (Behavior) demonstrates superior knowledge in scientific and humane techniques to address behavior health, problem prevention, training, management, and behavior modification.

# ABOUT THE AUTHORS

### *Kenneth M. Martin, DVM*

Dr. Martin is the owner of Veterinary Behavior Consultations, LLC, a veterinary clinic with practice limited to the prevention and treatment of animal behavior disorders. He graduated from Louisiana State University, School of Veterinary Medicine in 1999. He practiced companion animal and exotic animal medicine and surgery, as well as emergency medicine prior to completing a behavior medicine residency at Purdue University's Animal Behavior Clinic. He is working toward diplomate status by the American College of Veterinary Behaviorists. Dr. Martin is a contributing author to the textbooks *Manual of Parrot Behavior* and *Animal Behavior for Veterinary Technicians and Nurses*. He frequently lectures at veterinary continuing education conferences and seminars. He guest lectures to veterinary medicine students at the LSU School of Veterinary Medicine. His professional interests include conflict-related (owner-directed) aggression, compulsive disorders, behavioral development, and psychopharmacology. He is a member of the American Veterinary Medical Association, Southeast Louisiana Veterinary Association, and the American Veterinary Society of Animal Behavior. Dr. Martin currently shares his home with two beloved Belgian Malinois, Iliana and Polo.

### *Debbie Martin, RVT, VTS (Behavior), CPDT-KA, KPA CTP*

Debbie is the animal behavior technician for Veterinary Behavior Consultations, LLC. Debbie has a B.S. from The Ohio State University in human ecology, and an associate of applied science degree in veterinary technology from Columbus State Community College. She has been a full time registered veterinary technician since 1996. She began instructing puppy socialization classes in 1997. Debbie is a Veterinary Technician Specialist (Behavior) and a professional member of the Society of Veterinary Behavior Technicians. Debbie is a certified professional dog trainer (CPDT-KA), Karen Pryor Academy Certified Training Partner (KPA CTP), and Karen Pryor Academy faculty member. She lectures at local and national veterinary conferences and universities to veterinary and veterinary technician students. Debbie is a published author in veterinary technician journals and is a contributing author in the textbook *Animal Behavior for Veterinary Technicians and Nurses*. Debbie currently shares her home with Iris, a beagle-terrier mix with one eye, and Jazmin, a Belgian Malinois.